To Ritva

CHINESE JADES

IN

THE AVERY BRUNDAGE COLLECTION

Second Revised Edition

By René-Yvon Lefebvre d'Argencé

ASIAN ART MUSEUM OF SAN FRANCISCO

This project is supported by a grant from The Museum Society, San Francisco.

Photography
by Joe Schopplein

Produced by Kodansha International

Library of Congress Catalogue Card Number 77-18358
1977
Printed in Japan
by Dai Nippon Printing Co., Ltd.

Contents

Acknowledgments

THE author of this book, Professor René-Yvon Lefebvre d'Argencé, is an authority on Jade, a subject which is so important in Chinese culture. He has also had the advantage of working for some years with one of the largest and most comprehensive collections of this fascinating mineral and jewel. His interest in the subject—uncommon to most U.S. museum directors and curators—was aroused years ago by contact with the late Dr. Salmony who was at the time preparing a monumental volume on Jade which, alas, was never finished.

Professor d'Argencé has given special attention to that more or less no-man's-land—the period of nearly 1500 years between the Han and Ch'ing dynasties—that has either been ignored by or defied the research of scholars.

When his studies have been completed, he hopes to be able to add something to the knowledge of this long period in the history of Jade carving which, as yet, is practically untouched by the experts.

While representative pieces have been selected it has unfortunately been impossible, in this volume, to illustrate more than 150 of the total of some 1200 items in the Collection.

Professor d'Argencé is the Director of the Asian Art Museum of San Francisco, a completely independent institution, housed in its own building which was specially designed and constructed to contain The Avery Brundage Collection. He has been the Director and Chief Curator for the past eleven years. After a world-wide search to find the right man to occupy this important position, Professor d'Argencé was found in Berkeley, where he was teaching at the University of California. His training for the position was ideal since he had been a Curator at the famous Cernuschi Museum in Paris, a member of the Ecole Francaise d'Extrême-Orient, and Director of museums in Saigon and Hanoi. Educated at the Sorbonne in Paris, and at Cambridge University in England, he had also studied in Vietnam, Taiwan and Japan. He is a distinguished linguist, familiar with the Chinese, Japanese and Vietnamese languages as well as English, French and Finnish.

Half of the interest of any collection depends on the method of its display, and Professor d'Argencé and his staff have a reputation for fine arrangements of the objects under their direction that has aroused praise in many quarters.

He has finished a number of handbooks on The Avery Brundage Collection and is now working on the permanent catalogue. Many articles and pamphlets on Oriental art have come from his pen. Professor d'Argencé loves the objects under his care and he has impeccable taste and a sharp eye. His assistance in the acquisitions since he became Director has been of tremendous value. San Francisco is fortunate to have him at the head of the Asian Art Museum.

AVERY BRUNDAGE
Chicago, May 1972

Chinese Jades is the fifth in a series of volumes presenting a cross section of the various departments of The Avery Brundage Collection. The items illustrated here represent approximately 10 percent of the holdings of a department which contains over 1200 objects and could probably furnish all the necessary material for a detailed history of the evolution of Chinese jades. Practically all the items that have been selected for this book are now on view in the Jade Room which was opened in 1969 at the Asian Art Museum as a result of the generosity of the Cyril Magnin Family.

As for all other volumes in the series our selection was based essentially on two criteria: esthetic quality and historical interest. Once again we have attempted to present this selection in a systematic and chronological order, inasmuch as this is feasible in a field where lacunae and incertitudes far exceed irrefutable landmarks. Such audacity has no other excuse than the desire to share with scholars and the general public alike the tremendous wealth of a still largely unknown collection.

Published in 1972 the first edition of this volume has been out of print for some time. This second, revised edition takes into account the archaeological discoveries of the past five years as well as recent scholarly publications on the subject. This has led us in a few instances to modify or refine some of our original datings.

I am deeply grateful to The Museum Society for sponsoring this publication. I am also indebted to all members of the staff of the Asian Art Museum for their indefatigable support—Messrs. David L. Smith and Anthony Garino have worked in close collaboration with Mr. Joseph Schopplein who was responsible for the photography and achieved wonders with a material which is by nature a photographer's nightmare; Mr. Fred Cline, the Librarian of the Museum prepared a comprehensive bibliography which was extremely helpful. He also kept abreast with my research by providing me with copies of rare books and by seeing to it that I would not miss any new publications that appeared occasionally, as my work was already well underway; Mrs. Jean Flockton typed the manuscript and Curators Sylvia Shangraw and Terese Tse Bartholomew offered many precious suggestions concerning its form and contents. In addition Diana Turner, Curator of Education, assisted in the editing of this second version of the book with her usual enthusiasm and efficiency.

René-Yvon Lefebvre d'Argencé
Director and Chief Curator
Asian Art Museum of San Francisco
The Avery Brundage Collection

Introduction

Nature and Contents of the Collection

THE Avery Brundage Collection comprises about twelve hundred pieces of carved jade, including a small number of Indian or Indian style objects (Pls. LXXIV to LXXVI) and two or three score of other semi-precious stones or comparable substances like lapis lazuli, quartz, turquoise, chalcedony (mainly agate and cornelian) chloromelanite, malachite, steatite (soap-stone), coral, amber and hornbill (Pls. LX, LXIV, LXXVII and LXXVIII).

In terms of sheer number, this is the second largest department in the collection, coming immediately after Chinese ceramics. Carefully selected over several decades of patient and systematic research, it ranks among the finest groups of jades ever assembled under one roof.

With the exception of ceramics, jade carving is the only art form to have remained creative during four thousand years of Chinese history, from the neolithic period to modern times. Unlike most other collections, ours illustrates all the major types and styles of this long history, including a numerous and most unusual group of objects, mostly animal figurines, dating from the Han to the Ming dynasty (Pls. XX through XXXVII). Particularly noted for its holdings in the two periods, which are generally regarded as lapidary peaks namely, the Warring States and the Ch'ien Lung periods, the collection is also unparalleled in three other areas — that of miniature mountains illustrating popular Buddhist or Taoist themes (Pls. LXIV through LXVII), that of rhytons (Pls. XXXIV, XXXVII, XLIX, LVII, LIX and LXXVII) and that of vessels imitating ancient bronze prototypes (Pls. XXXVI, XXXVIII, L, LII through LVI, LVIII, LX and LXXIV).

Nature and Main Sources of Chinese Jade

As early as 1863 the French scientist, Alexis Damour, established that our word jade or its Chinese counterpart *yü* are loose terms, which designate at least two very different types of stones: nephrite and jadeite. Nephrite, a silicate of calcium and magnesium, is a mineral of fibrous structure, which belongs to the amphibole group. Jadeite, a silicate of sodium and aluminium, has a cryptocrystalline structure and belongs to the pyroxene group of minerals. Jadeite is the harder of the two and has a higher specific gravity. It can also take a higher or more glossy polish, the lustre of polished nephrite being somewhat oily without ever having the sticky appearance of steatite, also known as soapstone. When free of any foreign elements, both nephrite and jadeite are colorless or white. Pure white nephrite is known as mutton-fat jade (*yang-chih-yü*), (Pl. LIII) a highly appreciated variety. Usually, however, both minerals exhibit a wide range of colors which are due to a variety of chemical elements, especially iron. Mottled and veined effects are quite frequent. The original colors of archaic jades have frequently been affected by prolonged contacts with earth chemicals or other organic substances (*Ko*-dagger of Pl. IV). Most have lost their translucency, many have turned brown, grey or even white as a result of advanced calcification. This last category is known as "chicken-bone white" (*chi-ku-pai*) (Pendant of Pl. XV) and is very esteemed by Chinese antiquarians. Some colors, like brilliant emerald green, apple green, snow white and mauve are typical of jadeite. Nephrite has a wide range of browns, greys and greens that are rarely found in jadeite. Despite all these chemical and physical differences, the two minerals cannot always be told from one another without the help of special laboratory equipment. As a rule, it can be assumed that jadeite did not reach Chinese workshops before the eighteenth century so that for all practical purposes, archaic, medieval, Ming and early Ch'ing jades are nephrite. All the objects illustrated in this book are nephrite unless otherwise specified.

To set collectors' hearts at ease, it should be added that both nephrite and jadeite are "true" jade so that the appurtenance of a given object to one group of minerals or the other has usually no bearing on the commercial value of the object in question.

Besides nephrite or jadeite, the only other mineral carved by Chinese lapidaries that could conceivably be accepted as true jade is chloromelanite, a term which was also invented by Damour. Chloromelanite, a variety of jadeite particularly rich in iron, can easily be told from both nephrite and jadeite because of its dull and dark green color. It was hardly used at all in China until late in the 19th century.

Jade has always fascinated the Chinese. It is the only precious or semi-precious stone to which they have paid unfailing respect throughout their long history. Already in Confucius' time, jade was the favorite stone of the perfect gentleman, because it embodied all the cardinal virtues. Its warm brilliance was likened to charity, its hardness to wisdom, the sharp yet harmless edges of its contours to justice. When shaped into girdle-pendants that looked as though they were falling to the ground, it suggested humbleness; when struck, music (a virtue in its own right). Its flaws, that are obvious without impairing its beauty, were compared to loyalty and its translucency and radiance to honesty.[1]

With time jade came to be associated in popular belief with everything that is noble, pure, beautiful and indestructible. Thus in contemporary Chinese a "jade person" is a lovely girl, a "jade heart" a pure heart, a "jade tree" a handsome and talented young man, etc.

The irresistible attraction that jade had and still has for the Chinese cannot be explained on such ethereal grounds only. There is something very earthly and sensuous about the stone itself, regardless of colors and shape. Naturally cool and soft to the touch, it warms up quickly when kept in the palm of the hand and gives a pleasant sensation, which is particularly appreciated by Chinese connoisseurs. Many small pieces, known as *pa wan* (hold and enjoy),[2] some shaped into recognizable objects, some with simple geometric forms, were made specifically to be fondled as much as to be looked at. The same unparalleled tactile characteristics of the stone also explain why until quite recently the best tea or rice bowls, the best chopsticks, the best pipe-stems, the best brush handles and many other high-quality objects of everyday use were made of jade. Besides, the Chinese have for many centuries attributed magical properties to the stone. It was used as a medicine and a talisman against diseases or accidents and after death against the decomposition of the corpse (Pl. XXIII).

It is all the more surprising to realize that there is no evidence textual or archeological that the jade stone was ever found in China proper or even in most neighboring countries with the exception of Burma. Throughout history the Chinese jade carvers received the raw material from quarries or river beds located in distant regions. Until quite recently the main, if not the only source of supply was the region of Khotan and Yarkand in present day Chinese Turkestan. The jadeite mines of Upper Burma were not exploited until the 18th century A.D. and the same is probably true of Siberian nephrite[3] which is noted for its distinctive spinach green variety (Pls. LVI, LXI, LXII, LXV, LXVIII).

Tools and Methods of Carving

Jade is harder than most metals including bronze, iron or commercial steel and harder than most minerals with the exception of diamond and quartz. Yet until quite recently jade was carved with such primitive tools as the wire saw and a variety of discs, wheels, drills and gouges made of steel and wrought iron. Most of these tools were operated on wooden lathes. Throughout the neolithic period and probably during many centuries of the Bronze Age period as well, most tools must have been made of wood, bone or sandstone.

Part of the mystery is due to the fact that jade was never really carved. Cutting tools were always used in conjunction with abrasives which did most of the work. Instead of our word "carving" the Chinese use the term "grinding and polishing" (cho mo) which describes more adequately the techniques involved. Until carborundum, a most potent product, was invented in the 20th century, workshops relied on a variety of natural abrasives, especially quartz powder, crushed garnets and corundum.

No technical device, however ingenious, will ever suffice to account for the splendor and sophistication of the best finished products. Dedication, patience and years of arduous training were the main assets of the jade carvers of China, a group of craftsmen whose skill and perfectionism were only equalled by those of the bronze casters of the Shang and Early Western Chou period. No wonder that quite a few of their most impressive masterpieces are frequently regarded as negligible or simply bizarre in societies where the values of speed, quantity and businesslike efficiency have superseded those of quality and durability and where perfectionism has become a rather derogative term.

Jadeology and The Dating of Jade Carvings

If jadeology is a science, it is a very new one. The epoch-making studies of Wu Ta-ch'eng for China and Berthold Laufer for the West can be regarded as the starting points of genuine scientific interest in the field. These books were dated respectively 1889 and 1912 and have been followed by no more than a score of serious studies on the subject, so that our understanding of Chinese jade carvings, of their use, meaning and stylistic development is far inferior to the one we have acquired in all other fields.

It must be recognized that the difficulties inherent in the material and the impossibility of studying it from reproductions are sufficient deterrents for most scholars who do not have access to a large comprehensive collection.

Jades are practically never signed or dated prior to the Ch'ien Lung period and even mid or late Ch'ing inscribed pieces are in the minority. Very few old texts have survived and those that are still available are either unreliable or deal with uses and symbolism rather than with the objects themselves. With the exception of a few pieces (see for instance Pls. IV and XIII through XVII), the vast majority of archaic and medieval jades appeared on the market as a result of uncontrolled excavations or of sales from old collections where no reliable records were kept. In this respect the bird, which is illustrated on plate XXIII and can be traced back to Wu Ta-ch'eng's collection, should be regarded as an exceptional windfall.

In the circumstances and pending new archeological evidence, the best and frequently only approach rests with a patient stylistic research based on close comparison with other media, such as bronze, ceramics or even sculpture, lacquer-ware and works in gold, silver, wood and cloisonné for the medieval and later periods. What makes this research so very slow and in some ways frustrating is that similarities are hard to come by, especially for the medieval and Ming periods. To a large extent jade carvers lived in a closed world and were not very receptive to external influences or current fashions. Essentially conservative, they could produce the same types of objects for generations and suddenly become daring innovators only to revert to old prototypes after a short period of time. It seems that they always served a specific taste, that of the well-to-do, who in China were generally members of the intelligentsia, and went on using the same tools for centuries. Whatever they borrowed from other artists or craftsmen was adapted to suit their own traditions and work habits.

Research of this kind cannot afford to let any stone remain unturned, so to speak. At this analytic phase of their study jadeologists are more concerned with revealing details and clues, however thin the latter may be, than with sweeping generalizations.

Thematic and Stylistic Developments

The preceding will, hopefully, make it clear that some of the contents of this section, especially those dealing with the medieval periods, should not be regarded as anything else than working hypotheses.

The history of Chinese jades can be tentatively divided into three main periods; the ancient, the medieval and the modern.

So far specialists have spent more time studying archaic jades than those of any other period. Reliable excavations, like those of An-yang (Pl. IV) or Chin-ts'un (Pls. XII and XIII) have shed considerable light on the provenance, dating and use of archaic jades and by a curious twist of history, have made them more accessible and familiar to the general public than those of more recent times. The initial stage of this ancient period coincides with the later stone age and is illustrated by very few animal sculptures (Pl. I). The second stage corresponds to the Shang, Western Chou and Ch'un-ch'iu periods. It is characterized by three main categories of objects: religious symbols, at times of large dimensions (Pl. II), insignia of rank in the shape of blades, frequently derived from utilitarian tools or weapons (Pls. III through V) and zoomorphic pendants or appliques generally carved out of small and thin slabs (Pls. VI through X). Many of these objects are plain; others are more or less heavily decorated with geometric motifs which recall those of contemporaneous bronze vessels, weapons or implements. The third stage overlaps the Warring States and Western Han periods. This was an age of daring experimentation and high technical achievements, which remained models of excellence for all generations to come and were only equalled two millennia later by some of the best products of the Ch'ien Lung period. This climax of the Chinese lapidary art is characterized by an ebullient calligraphic rhythm, which manifests itself in curvilinear contours of great audacity (Pls. XIII, XV, XVIII) and close-knit ornamental schemes based mainly on variations of the spiral (Pls. XIII and XIV). Here also many shapes and motifs of decoration were borrowed or derived from contemporaneous bronzes. The objects produced during this period are generally small with the exception of *pi, ts'ung* or other symbols of rank, and form three main groups: zoomorphic or quasi-zoomorphic pendants and beads with a large proportion of dragons and birds (these are still made from thin slabs of jade, viz. Pls. XIII through XV), ornaments for the warrior's equipment (Pls. XIV and XVI) and, another innovation, anthropomorphic pendants which are remarkably plain and static when compared to their zoomorphic counterparts (Pls. XIX and XX). Modest as it is, this first appearance of human representations can hardly be overemphasized because it reflects drastic changes in religious practises that so far had been exclusively concerned with animals or animal spirits. Thematically speaking, this is also a major turning point in what has been called elsewhere the Chinese artist's gradual conquest of the universe.[4]

Few are the objects that can be dated late Han with any degree of certainty. In this book the first two centuries of our era have consequently been treated as a sort of transitional phase leading to the medieval period. Small animal figurines in the round, often carved out of very dark or even blackish jade, and contrasting vividly with archaic zoomorphs, seem to form the main contribution of the period (Pls. XXII through XXIV). Studied from life, these animals, many of them domestic or tame, do not exhibit any of the complex ornamental schemes that were so typical of the ancient period, nor do they seem to reflect any religious overtones with perhaps the exception of cicadas or similar pieces used to close the apertures of the body after death (Pl. XXIII). With this group of animals the art of jade carving enters its naturalistic phase which, of course, can be interpreted as another facet of the humanizing tendencies noted in connection with the last stage of the ancient period.

The medieval period proper lasted for approximately twelve hundred years from the 3rd to the 14th century—a big chunk of Chinese history and certainly the least known where jade is concerned. Here the student cannot even rely on a few controlled excavations or on comparisons with other materials. Practically all finds were due to chance or pilfering and analogies with other types of objects are harder to come by as jade carvers become more conscious of the intrinsic potentialities of their material. Most museums and collectors have refrained from acquiring objects attributed to the period and most writers have dealt with them with no more than a few casual remarks. Prudence might have prompted us to follow the same course of action had it not been for the fact that Avery Brundage, whose taste was never confined to current fashions or limited by scholastic prejudices, collected a large number of objects attributable to the period in question. On stylistic grounds these twelve centuries, which correspond to the first truly sculptural trend in the history of Chinese jades and simultaneously to their last formative phase, can be divided into three consecutive stages: the early medieval stage corresponding approximately to the 3rd, 4th, 5th and 6th centuries, the mid medieval stage, spanning four hundred years, from the 7th to the 10th century and the late medieval stage, which accounts for the next four hundred years, from the 11th to the 14th century. Needless to say, this chronology is offered for its relative rather than absolute value and will probably remain subject to adjustments for several decades to come. The initial stage of the period produced essentially two types of objects: animal figurines in the round and a few types of receptacles. At first the animal figurines retained a good deal of the Han spirit (Pls. XXV and XXVI) and then gradually divorced themselves from it as they began to illustrate a whole menagerie of mythical beasts with, frequently, caricatural overtones (Pls. XXVII through XXIX). The emergence of such fabulous creatures which, incidentally, set the tone for many hybrids of all subsequent periods, reflects on the one hand a renewed interest for ancient mythology and consequently for the tenets of the oldest religious beliefs, and on the other hand strong anti-Buddhistic feelings which, as we know, were deeply rooted among the intelligentsia of the period. The main type of receptacles to be noted consists of a group of zoomorphs similar to those we have just described, but hollowed out and equipped with stoppers (Pl. XXIX). Just as Han and early medieval carvers had at first reacted violently against the Warring States approach, the carvers of the mid medieval period began by rejecting almost all the dreams or nightmares of their immediate predecessors. They reverted to the naturalistic tendencies of the Han carvers and brought them to their logical conclusion (Pls. XXXI and XXXII). Later on, however, they produced at least two types of revolutionary containers, one which was directly inspired by contemporaneous metallic or ceramic models (Pl. XXXV) and another one which reveals a keen antiquarian interest usually centered on Warring States prototypes (Pl. XXX). The same antiquarian spirit, but now gradually enriched by borrowings from the earliest periods of the Bronze Age, as well as from the Warring States, seems to pervade the last stage of the medieval period (Pls. XXXVI through XXXVIII). Towards the 14th century, however, a few items with unprecedented anecdotic and symbolic overtones foreshadow one of the most important trends of the modern period.

The Ming and early Ch'ing dynasties' main contribution to the glyptic art of China seems to rest with new sculptural concepts. Human beings and plants (Pls. XLII through XLVI) play an increasingly important part alongside of animal statuettes, which are still in the majority. All these figurines are larger and bulkier than before. Their robust, rounded volumes are enhanced by warm, waxy surfaces. Quadrupeds, fish and even birds are frequently shown together with embryos of landscape settings (Pls. XLIV, XLV) and, for the first time, quadrupeds stand on their four legs instead of being in reclining or crouching positions (Pls. XLIII and XLIV). Most of these statuettes were made as auspicious and humorous gifts that are charged with a new kind of symbolism, frequently based on puns and rebuses (Pls. XLII through XLVIII). Simultaneously archaistic vessels continue to be made in very much the same vein as before. They pretend to be miniature imitations of ancient bronze vessels, but in most instances are hardly more than three-dimensional renderings of usually inaccurate line drawings (Pls. XXXVIII and L).

The second stage of the modern period corresponds to the 18th century A.D. when China was ruled by Emperor Ch'ien Lung whose enthusiasm and strong esthetic convictions were largely responsible for bringing the art of jade carving to a long-awaited maturity. This period of unsurpassable achievements was marked by two outstanding features: eclecticism and technical virtuosity. One important aspect of this eclecticism, which was a reflection of the emperor's own taste, coincided with the third and main wave of archaism since the medieval period (Pls. LII through LVI and LVIII through LX). Unlike their predecessors who worked from line drawings, 18th century carvers had access to the ancient bronze vessels of the imperial collection. Usually, however, their products were not servile imitations of these vessels. They stand out as marvels of fully integrated anachronisms where modern elements are carefully blended with those belonging to various stages of the ancient period. The most successful of these transpositions and juxtapositions were expressions of a highly original idiom, often based on a new calligraphic approach, and rank among the very best carvings of any period (Pls. LII through LVI). The eclectic mood which pervaded the 18th century also manifested itself in daring innovations with little or no ties with the past. For instance, particular attention was paid to the making of a variety of objects destined to the writer's desk, including brush holders (Pls. LXI and LXIII), miniature mountains (Pls. LXIV through LXVIII) and table screens (Pls. LXVIII). Many of these objects were decorated with religious scenes in settings inspired by contemporaneous landscape paintings. Human figurines, too, whether religious or profane, are now made in large quantities and can attain considerable dimensions (Pl. LXXIII). Of particular interest is a series of lohans represented as hermits meditating in their mountainous retreats.

This is also the time when Chinese workshops, prompted by the court, became receptive to a taste which can be traced back to 17th century India. This taste is at the origin of the carving of extremely thin, almost transparent and, at times, reticulated vessels with ornamental schemes that are essentially floral and rigidly symmetrical (Plates LXXIV through LXXVI). Finally the same eclectic leanings explain that some of the best carvers began to include the use of a wide variety of other stones or stone-like substances. Particularly in favor were lapis lazuli (Pls. LX, LXIV and LXVI), turquoise, coral (Pl. LXXVII) and several kinds of chalcedony, including agate and cornelian (Pls. LXXVII and LXXIX) which all offered colors and shades of colors rarely or never found in nephrite or jadeite.

Despite this intense activity and the imperial patronage that largely accounts for it, jade carvings remained for the most part just as anonymous as before. The couple of names or so of master carvers that have passed to posterity cannot be related to any known object. However, quite a few of the most elegant pieces of the period are incised with Ch'ien Lung marks or more or less poetical inscriptions, some of which also bear Ch'ien Lung's seals (Pls. LIX and LXIV).

The 19th century and the first three quarters of the 20th century can be regarded as a post Ch'ien Lung period in the sense that they have not been able to free themselves from the tremendous weight of the 18th century's tradition (Pls. LXXIX and LXXX). When new currents can be noted they seem slightly retrograde. This is, for instance, the first time that almost exact replicas of ancient bronze vessels have been made in jade without the slightest touch of imagination. This, of course, does not augur well for the future of the now four thousand years old art form; and yet, if technical excellence can be preserved, nothing is lost. In jade, probably more than in any other medium, artistic genius has always been intimately linked with manual dexterity.

Jade and Symbolism

There is hardly any piece of Chinese jade which is not replete with symbolic connotations. Needless to say, the symbols involved have varied considerably from one period to the other. One curious aspect of modern research is that a great deal of time and effort have been spent in the study, often resulting in a wild goose chase, of the most ancient symbols when those, much more accessible, of the later periods have been almost entirely neglected. No doubt, much remains to be done on this subject, particularly in that still virgin field of the medieval period. We have, however, endeavored here to alleviate some of the most glaring shortcomings by emphasizing the fact that many a piece that looks outwardly like no more than an elegant and imaginative group of animals, plants or objects does, in fact, carry a message that reached directly the heart and soul of the person for whom it was made. In this sense, jade carving unveils more than any other medium many essential aspects of Chinese psychology and art appreciation.

(1) *Book of Rites*, *P'ing-i* f 2
(2) Also known as "finger pieces" or "fondling pieces" (the latter term coined by S. Howard Hansford)
(3) Hansford, *Jade, Essence of Hills and Streams*
(4) d'Argencé, *A.B.C. Chinese Treasures*, p. 9

Plate I

RESTING BIRD

Mottled green with white patches
Neolithic period (ca. 1700 B.C.)
L. 3 1/8 in. H. 2 in.   B60 J331

This bird, shaped from a river pebble, is the earliest jade in the collection.   With the exception of the head and neck, the contours of the "finished" product seems to follow closely those of the original stone.   Wings and legs are outlined by rounded depressions, while the neck is defined by a circular one.   The smoothness of the surface is interrupted in only two places, the mouth which is marked by a shallow slit and the underside of the legs where incisions suggest claws.

Published: Salmony, *Chinese Jade,* Pl. II-3; d'Argencé, *Asia Foundation,* Pl. II and *A.B.C. Chinese Treasures,* Pl. 35

Plate II

PI and *TS'UNG*

Off-white with iron rust patches, and light green with black markings
Respectively Neolithic or Early Shang dynasty (ca. 16th century B.C.*) and Warring States*
period (5th-3rd century B.C.*)*
Diameter of Pi, 6 in. Height of Ts'ung 6 in.   *B60 J908 and B60 J20+*

In the West the *pi* is usually described as a "perforated disc" and the *Ts'ung* as a
"tube within a cube" or a "square outside and round inside".   In Chinese literature
the terms have been in use since at least the 3rd or 2nd century B.C. and a famous
Han text indicates that an azure *pi* would symbolize Heaven, while a yellowish
brown *ts'ung* was a symbol of Earth.[1]   Regardless of whether or not the symbolic
values of such objects were accepted in more ancient times, there is little doubt
that at least *pi* shapes with wide central apertures were known as early as the
neolithic period.[2] Two large areas on the outer rim of the *pi* have turned opaque
as a result of extensive calcification, which may have been caused by prolonged
contact with some organic substance during burial.

(1)   See the commentary of the *Chou Li* by Cheng K'ang-cheng and in the *Chou Li* itself
      chapter V/17a.
(2)   See for instance *K'ao Ku Hsüeh Pao* 1954, no. 7, Pl. 3, fig. 1 and *Wen Wu* 1972, no. 2, p. 26, fig. 3.

Plate III

KO-DAGGER with bronze handle

Mottled tan with patches of green
Late Shang period (13th-11th century B.C.)
L. 10 1/8 in.   *B60 J907*

Ritual blades like this one and those of the next plate can be traced back to stone or bronze prototypes. They were essentially symbolic tokens derived from utilitarian tools or weapons.

The *ko*, a dagger-axe typical of the Chinese Bronze Age, was mounted on a wooden shaft set at right angles. Early specimens had off-center tangs. The hole in the middle of the tang and the spurs, at its lower part, served to secure the blade to the shaft by means of thongs.

The countersunk *t'ao-t'ieh* masks of the bronze handle were probably inlaid with turquoise or some other semi-precious stone.[1]

(1) Cf. d'Argencé, *A.B.C. Bronzes*, Pl. XXIII. See also Hansford, *Jade, Essence of Hills and Streams*, Pl. A38 for a similar example in the Oertzen collection or again Loehr, *Ancient Chinese Jades*, no. 75.

PLATE IV

AXE

Off-white with brown markings
Late Shang period (13th–11th century B.C.*)*
H. 6 1/4 in.   *B60 J515*

This type of flat axe, with or without decoration, is also quite characteristic of the Chinese Bronze Age and numerically speaking second only to *ko*-daggers.[1]

Both sides of this rare specimen, which was excavated in An-yang itself, present a series of deep longitudinal grooves separated by rounded ridges. The short, recessed tang is perforated with a large attachment hole, which was drilled all the way through from one side. The cutting edge of the blade slopes from both sides.

Published: Umehara, *Anyō no Kenkyū*, Kyoto, 1941, Pl. 39–2 and *Shina Ko-gyoku Zuroku*, Tokyo, 1955, Pl. XXVI
(1) See Pl. III.

KO-DAGGER

Mottled brown with spots of calcification on one side
Late Shang or Early Western Chou period (13th–10th century B.C.*)*
L. 11 1/4 in.   *B60 J16 +*

This example is more removed from utilitarian prototypes than the dagger-axe of the preceding plate. The blade ends in spurs with slight indentations. The upper edge of the tang is serrated and the attachment hole was drilled all the way through from one side. One side of the blade shows a slightly discolored semicircular halo. This very unusual feature is, in fact, the "shadow" of a perforated disc of the *pi*-type,[1] which must have remained many centuries in direct contact with the blade.

Published: d'Argence, *Propyläen*, Pl. 8a
(1) See Pl. II.

SWORD

Grey-green with purple and black markings
Early Western Chou period (ca. 10th century B.C.*)*
L. 12 1/2 in.   *B60 J511*

The grip of this remarkably thin ceremonial sword ends in two small slanted spurs. The cutting edge of the blade is bevelled on one side only and the attachment hole was drilled from one side also. The upper edge of the tang is slightly damaged.

Published: Huang Chün, *Ku Yü T'u Lu Ch'u Chi*, Peking 1939, vol. 1, Pl. 14

PLATE V

FINIAL

Grey-green with brown markings
Late Shang period (13th–11th century B.C.*)*
L. 2 5/8 in.   *B60 J702*

The upper half of a perforated disc constitutes the arched body of a dragon with projecting head and tail. The base of the disc is equipped with a rectangular extension with two attachment holes indicating that the finial may have served as a standard or staff top. Few insignia of rank of this kind can be ascribed such an early date. The dragon is typical of the period. The disproportionately large head has a gaping mouth with a pair of fangs and a turned-up nose. The bottle-shaped horn and the curling tail are free-sculptured. The flanks are decorated with a series of large barbed-scale motifs. The thin back is incised with a zigzag pattern and the tail with a design of coiled feathers, not unlike those of a rooster. Two short legs are tucked under the body.

Published: Loo, *Chinese Archaic Jades,* Pl. XVII, fig. 6; Salmony, *Carved Jade,* Pl. XXI, fig. 5; Na Chih-liang, *Yü Ch'i T'ung Shih,* Pl. 84, fig. 1

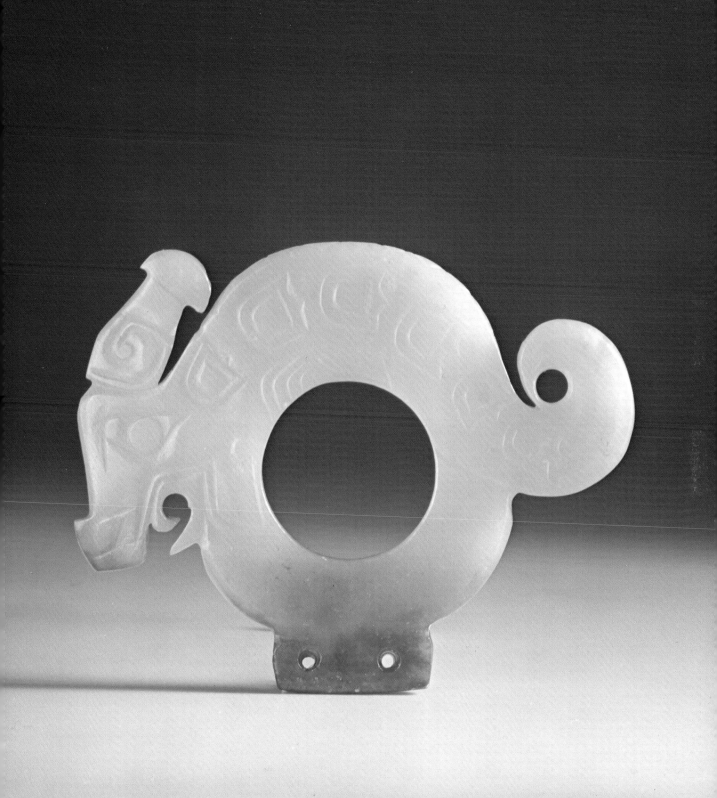

PLATE VI

PENDANTS IN SHAPE OF DRAGONS AND FELINES
Late Shang period
(13th-11th century B.C.*)*

ARCHED BROWN DRAGON[1] *L. 4 1/8 in.*	*B60 J658*
CROUCHING BLACK AND GREEN TIGER[2] *L. 3 in.*	*B60 J677*
CRAWLING LIGHT GREEN DRAGON L. 2 3/4 in.	*B60 J916*
GREY TIGER L. 2 3/4 in.	*B60 J538*
WHITE T'AO-T'IEH MASK[3] *H. 1 1/8 in.*	*B60 J805*

Late Shang or Early Western Chou pendants are exclusively zoomorphic and mostly made of small and thin slabs. In this early group the animals are, with the exception of the frontal *t'ao-t'ieh* mask, shown in profile with their legs close to their bodies and their heads close to the ground, as though they were crawling or scenting their prey. They are treated in a two dimensional manner, both sides of the slabs reproducing identical features. Only the *t'ao-t'ieh* mask has a plain back.

There is frequently a striking analogy between these jade animals and those which appear on the surface of contemporaneous bronze vessels and implements.

Composite or fantastic species are numerous and are usually characterized by a profusion of minute details done in simple incisions, double lines, raised lines or low relief.

The dragons and the mask have bottle-shaped horns and the shapes of the tails of the dragons reveal that they may have served as cutting or piercing tools.

Published: B60 J658: d'Argencé, *Apollo,* p. 135, fig. 1; B60 J677: Loo, *Chinese Archaic Jades,* Pl. XVII, fig. 4; Rawson and Ayers, *Chinese Jade,* no. 60; B60 J538: d'Argencé, *A.B.C. Chinese Treasures,* fig. 37.

(1) See *Wen Wu* 1972, no. 8, p. 24, fig. 1 and *K'ao Ku* 1976, no. 4, p. 269, fig. 1, no. 9 and Pl. 8, no. 6 for two Late Shang comparable specimens, one of them excavated at An-yang in 1975.

(2) A similar piece was excavated from a Late Shang tomb at Ta-ssu-k'ung, An-yang in 1953 (See *K'ao Ku Hsüeh Pao,* Vol. 9, 1955, Pl. 17, fig. 1).

(3) A mask closely resembling this one was discovered in 1975 in the same Late Shang tomb mentioned above (See *K'ao Ku* 1976, no. 4, Pl. 8, no. 11 and p. 269, fig. 11, no. 5).

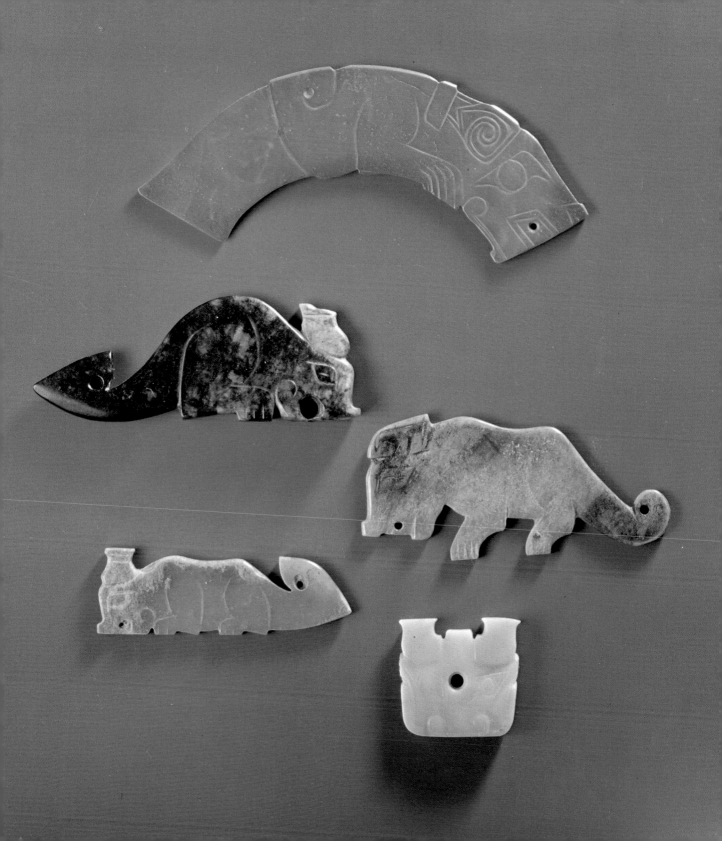

P<small>LATE</small> VII

BIRD AND FISH PENDANTS

From Late Shang to Early Western Chou period
(13th- 10th century B.C.)

GREY-GREEN CRESTED BIRD WITH FLEDGLING, Late Shang (*second row, right*)
H. 2 1/4 in.   *B60 J700*
FLATTENED OWL, calcified, Late Shang or Early Western Chou (second row, left)
L. 2 in.   *B60 J818*
GREY-GREEN FISH, Late Shang or Early Western Chou (bottom) [1]
L. 4 7/8 in.   *B60 J693*
MOTTLED TAN BIRD WITH FISH TAIL, partly calcified [2]
Late Shang or Early Western Chou (top)
L. 3 3/4 in.   *B60 J698*
CORMORANT, tan, partly calcified, Early Western Chou (*second row, center*)
L. 1 3/8 in.   *B60 J632*

Three of these birds belong to the same general stylistic group with the felines of the preceding plate. They are characterized by boldly undercut contours and a multiplicity of details frequently derived from basic geometric figures. These are not ordinary birds either. One, equipped with an oversized crenellated crest, carries its fledgling on its back. Another has a bottle-shaped head and the body of a fish with a parted tail and a couple of fins. The third one, more readily identifiable, is an owl. Owls played a prominent role in the mythology of ancient China, but their symbolic significance at such an early date, remains highly conjectural.

In contrast with these fabulous and somewhat redoubtable species, the fourth bird, i.e. the cormorant, and the fish exemplify a gentle group which, as can be seen here and in the next plate, consists mainly of birds, fishes, small animals and insects.

Published: B60 J700: Loo, *Chinese Archaic Jades,* Pl. XXIX, fig. 6; B60 J698: Loo, *Chinese Archaic Jades,* Pl. XXX, fig. 8; d'Argencé, *Apollo,* p. 135, fig. 1 (e); B60 J632: d'Argencé, *Apollo,* p. 135, fig. 1 (b); *Chinese Art Treasures,* fig. 38
(1) See *K'ao Ku* 1976, no. 4, p. 258, fig. 21, nos. 1 and 2 and Pl. 4, figs. 1 and 2 for Early Western Chou examples.
(2) Two Early Western Chou birds of this type were discovered near Peking in 1973/1974 (See *K'ao Ku* 1974, no. 5, p. 318, fig. 16, nos. 5 and 6).

PLATE VIII

TIGER HEAD

Mottled light green with brown and black markings, calcified in parts
Late Shang period (13th–11th century B.C.*) L. 1 1/8 in.   B60 J716*

TIGER

Mottled light green
Late Shang period (13th–11th century B.C.*)*
L. 2 in.   *B60 J794*

Beside flat pendants, Shang and Early Western Chou carvers also produced a relatively small group of zoomorphic subjects in the round. Most of them are diminutive figurines or heads. Many have perforations, which seem to indicate that they, too, were utilized as pendants or appliques.

The tiger head could also be described as a *t'ao-t'ieh* mask, but in contrast with the usually flat masks, this one has a lower jaw, two pairs of fangs and two stump legs. Certain authors believe that certain types of *t'ao-t'ieh* masks derive from tiger masks. Such three dimensional objects seems to support this theory.

The head and body of the crawling tiger[1] are covered with the familiar, partly realistic, partly conventionalized patterns, whereas the curved tail which tapers to a point, was left quite plain. The object may have served as a puncher or a stylet.

Published: B60 J716: d'Argencé, *A.B.C. Chinese Treasures,* fig. 36

(1) A similar tiger, but carved out of a piece of stone was discovered in a Late Shang tomb at An-yang in 1975 (See *K'ao Ku* 1976, no. 4, p. 269, fig. 11, no. 3 and Pl. 7, fig. 2 (left).

PLATE IX

DEER, HARE, PRAYING MANTIS, TURTLE, TOAD AND SALAMANDER PENDANTS

Western Chou period (10th–8th century B.C.)

DEER, green with brown markings, Western Chou (10th–8th century B.C.)
L. 3 1/16 in. B60 J849

HARE,[1] *mottled light grey, Early Western Chou (ca. 10th century B.C.)*
L. 7/8 in. B60 J573

PRAYING MANTIS, dark green, Western Chou (10th–8th century B.C.)
L. 1 1/4 in. B60 J633

TURTLE, greyish green, calcified in parts, Early Western Chou (ca. 10th century B.C.)
L. 2 1/4 in. B60 J808

SALAMANDER, tan, partly calcified, Western Chou (10th–8th century B.C.)
L. 2 3/8 in. B62 J33

TOAD, ivory color, partly calcified, Western Chou period (10th–8th century B.C.)
L. 1 1/8 in. B60 J894

By comparison with the fantastic and hybrid creatures of the preceding plates, this group looks refreshingly natural. With the exception of the turtle, whose shell sports a whorl circle in the best Shang tradition,[2] the animals are rendered realistically. The bodies are quite plain or at least deprived of conventional or symbolic linear schemes. They, nevertheless, convey a feeling of condensed, latent energy, which is due partly to lively postures, frequently suggesting suspended or incipient motion, and partly to the wide staring eyes, which give an unusual intensity to their facial expressions. It is not impossible that such objects were primarily expensive articles for personal adornment.

Published: B60 J849: d'Argencé, *Apollo,* p. 135, fig. 1 (d); B60 J573: d'Argencé, *Apollo,* p. 135, fig. 1 (a); B62 J33: d'Argencé, *A.B.C. Chinese Treasures,* fig. 39
(1) See *Wen Wu* 1972, no. 7, p. 7, fig. 9, no. 3 for a comparable example.
(2) See Hansford, *Jade, Essence of Hills and Streams,* Pl. A70 for a similar piece.

PLATE X

HUMAN MASK PENDANT

Light green
Western Chou or Ch'un-ch'iu period (10th-6th century B.C.)
H. 1 1/2 in. *B60 J726*

DRAGON PENDANT

Light green with brown and black patches
Western Chou or Ch'un-ch'iu period (10th-6th century B.C.)
L. 5 1/4 in. *B60 J811*

These pendants belong to a small and little known category with marked thematic and stylistic features. The contours of these anthropomorphic and, more rarely, zoomorphic pendants or ornaments undulate with so much flexibility that they, at times, suggest the folds of some soft material. Postures, too, can be highly distorted, as well illustrated by the dragon with its head turned all the way back. The contours are doubled by a continuous line in thread relief. Details, too, are rendered in thread relief and rely almost exclusively on curved lines, most of them ending in spirals.

Facial expressions are ferocious and, in the case of human masks, almost demoniac. They are characterized by an aquiline nose, two rows of bare teeth, large ears with pierced lobes and very big eyes with protruding globes. Alfred Salmony thought these features could correspond to the description of a mountain demon listed in the *Shan Hai Ching*.[1]

(1)   Salmony, *Chinese Jade*, p. 91

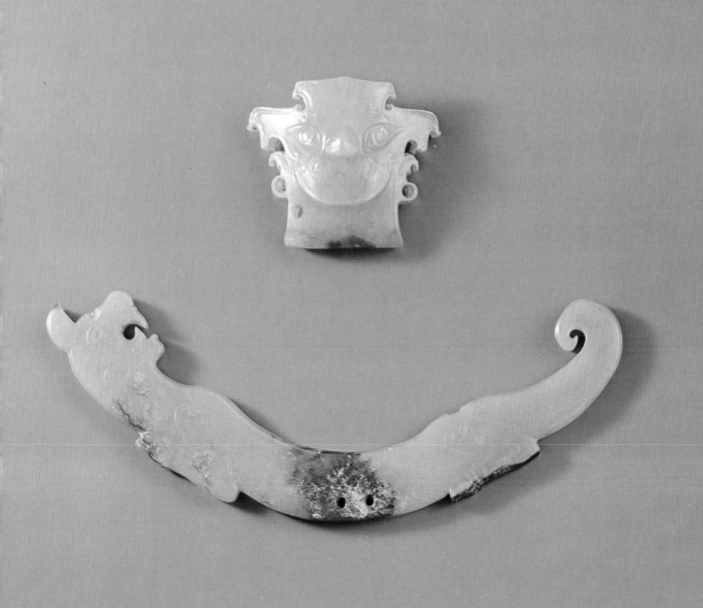

PLATE XI

TS'UNG

Amber with brown markings
Chou period (10th–3rd century B.C.*)*
Diam. 3 5/8 in.   *B60 J603*

This is the best preserved in a small group of *ts'ung* with human masks, which for lack of unquestionable dating criteria, have been ascribed to various segments of the Chou period.[1]   All these masks display the following characteristics: horizontal bands of striations on the forehead, large circular eyes with slit corners, no nose bridge to speak of, but pronounced nostrils, no mouth or lower jaw.

(1)   Cf. Pl. II.

PLATE **XII**

TIGER PENDANT

Ivory color, calcified
Warring States, Chin-ts'un style (ca. 3rd century B.C.)
L. 4 3/8 in. *B62 J63*

ARCHED PENDANT and *RECTANGULAR PLAQUE*

Green with brown patches
Late Ch'un-ch'iu or early Warring States period (5th century B.C.)
L. 3 1/2 in. for both objects. *B60 J528 and 566*

Between the relief borders of the two-headed tiger pendant, the field is decorated with incised C-shaped spirals and double lines according to a strictly symmetrical arrangement. Eyes, cheeks, beards and manes are also incised, while lower jaws are marked by rows of fine comb-hatching.

The other arched pendant and the plaque are excellent illustrations of the ebullient rhythm and close-knit ornamental schemes, which are so typical of the nascent Warring States style, regardless of media and workshops.[1] Animal shapes and elements organized around eye motifs are so intimately interlaced with geometrical patterns that they can hardly be told from one another.

Published: d'Argencé, *A.B.C. Chinese Treasures,* Pl. 40

(1) Similar objects were excavated from a 5th century tomb at Feng-shui-ling in Ch'ang-chih city in 1972 (See *K'ao Ku Hsüeh Pao* 1974, no. 2, Pl. 6, fig. 1 and Pl. 10, fig. 4).

PLATE XIII

DRAGON PENDANTS

Mottled green altered in parts
Warring States period, Chin-ts'un style
(ca. 3rd century B.C.)
L. 5 1/4 in. and 3 3/8 in.   B60 J675 and 665

Comparable silhouettes have been excavated at Chin-ts'un near Lo-yang in Honan province.[1]   The body of the larger dragon forms a double S ending in a bifurcated tail.   Each bend is accentuated by a curved or spiraling projection and the largest of these projections, just below the neck, is suggestive of a bird's head. The body proper is covered with a rather disorganized pattern of incised spirals, whereas the head, tail and projections are mostly striated.

The smaller pendant is less contorted, and the details of its silhouette were executed with utmost care.

Dragon plaques of this type may have served as insets for gold or gilt bronze belt-hooks, as can be seen in a few excavated pieces.

Published: B60 J665: Loo, *Chinese Archaic Jades,* Pl. XLV, fig. 7 and Rawson and Ayers, *Chinese Jade,* no. 116

(1) See S. Umehara, *Rakuyō Kinson Kobo Shūei,* Kyoto,1936, Pls. LXXXIX and XC, another Honan site where such pieces have been unearthed is that of Ch'ang-t'ai-kuan, Hsin-yang hsien (See *Wen Wu Ts'an K'ao Tz'u Liao* 1957, no. 9, p. 24, figs. 10 and 11).

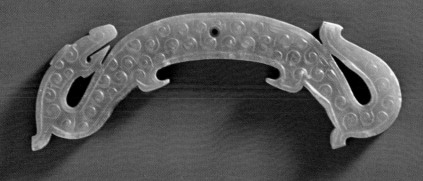

PLATE XIV

SWORD ORNAMENTS
Late Warring States period (ca. 3rd century B.C.*)*

GUARD   (*top*)
Ivory color with brown markings
L. 1 15/16 in.   B60 J561
INSETS FOR POMMELS (*second row*)
Light green and ivory color
Diam. 1 15/16 in. and 1 5/8 in.   B60 J621 *and* 803
SCABBARD BUCKLE   (*third row*)
Ivory color with brown markings
L. 2 15/16 in.   B60 J736
CHAPES   (*bottom*)
Light green and dark green, partly calcified
H. 1 7/8 in. and 1 3/16 in.   B62 J32 *and* B60 J567

Warring States carvers devised an important group of decorative jades for the archer's and swordsman's equipment.   They were keen on putting an impeccable finish to their products.   This is best seen in the manner they reserved some areas in their ornamental schemes for hair-thin and remarkably regular striations or hatchings, which recall certain technical patterns used in contemporaneous gold-smithing.

Both sides of the guard are identical with central motifs probably derived from the *t'ao-t'ieh* mask of former ages (see, for instance Pl. VI).[1]

The central zone of the larger pommel inset looks like an elaborate version of the whorl circle of earlier periods (see, for instance, the turtle of Pl. IX).[2]   The center of the other inset is occupied by a five-petalled rosette.   It would seem that floral motifs were not used in any significant quantity prior to the Warring States.

The scabbard buckle is decorated with a feline, which was to become a much favored motif of all subsequent periods.   This is a "cat derivation", as Salmony used to put it, with, at times, a bifurcated tail and a crest.   For the Chinese, this animal, is known as *ch'ih* and is said to be a hornless, immature dragon.

The smaller of the chápes is adorned on both sides with a highly conventional-ized monster's mask, while the central field of the other is filled with a spiralled grain pattern.

(1) Cf. also Hansford, *Jade, Essence of Hills and Streams*, Pl. B51.

(2) See *K'ao Ku T'ung Hsün* 1958, no. 9, Pl. 4, no. 4 for a similar piece found in a late Warring States tomb near Ch'ang-sha, Hunan province.

PLATE XV

GROUP OF ORNAMENTS

PERFORATED DISC AND RAMPANT DRAGONS   (right)
Light green, altered in parts
Warring States or Western Han period (ca. 3rd century B.C.)
W. 2 1/4 in.   B60 J742

Starting from the Warring States period, perforated discs are sometimes surmounted by an openwork plaque which consists of one or several dragons in a setting of cloud-shaped volutes. In this unusual object the dragons are positioned symmetrically on the lower section of the disc and with their backs attached to its rim.

PINHEAD IN SHAPE OF BIRD   (top)
Green with patches of brown, altered in parts
Warring States period (5th-3rd century B.C.)
H. 1 1/2 in.   B60 J815

The body of this peacock derivation is covered with conventionalized feathers which are also present on two branches of the tripartite tail. The bird has no wings, but carries on its back a curious appendage which is suggestive of diminutive wings.

FITTING IN SHAPE OF BIRD   (bottom)
Ivory color, partly calcified
Warring States period (5th-3rd century B.C.)
L. 1 1/8 in.   B60 J807

A few similar fittings or pendants were unearthed at the well-known site of Chin-ts'un near Lo-yang in Honan province.[1] Chin-ts'un jades are noted for the quality of their workmanship. Local artists seem to have taken great delight in producing little tours de force of unprecedented sophistication. Curvilinear contours of surprising audacity are combined with openwork features and extremely fine details. Here the front part of a crested bird is attached to a highly conventionalized leaf-shaped body. The tenon that juts out from the breast of the bird was probably inserted into some kind of solid material.

PENDANT   (left)
Ivory color, calcified
Late Warring States or Western Han period (ca. 3rd century B.C.)
L. 3 3/4 in.   B60 J679

A number of Warring States pendants look like knives, punchers or stylets with a zoomorphic or semi-zoomorphic handle. This particularly elegant item shows the silhouette of a dragon rising from the waves in a setting of spiraling clouds.[2]

Published: B60 J742: Loo, *Chinese Archaic Jades*, Pl. XLV, fig. 1; B60 J185: Salmony, *Chinese Jade*, Pl. XX-2 with an erroneous provenance; B60 J 679: Loo, *Chinese Archaic Jades*, Pl. LIII, fig. 9; Rawson and Ayers, *Chinese Jade*, no. 128
(1) See Pl. XIII. Compare also Hansford, *Jade, Essence of Hills and Streams*, Pl. B37.
(2) Compare with the dragons surmounting a 2nd century *pi* discovered at Man-ch'eng, Hopei province. (See *K'ao Ku* 1972, no. 1, p. 13, fig. 9).

Plate XVI

BELT-HOOKS

UPPER RIGHT, *Light green with traces of cinnabar red*
Warring States or Western Han period (5th–1st century B.C.*)*
H. 2 3/8 in.   *B60 J453*
UPPER LEFT, *Light green with brown markings*
Warring States period (5th–3rd century B.C.*)*
H. 1 5/8 in.   *B62 J40*
BELOW, *ivory color with brown markings*
Late Warring States or Early Western Han period (ca. 3rd century B.C.*)*
L. 4 5/16 in.   *B60 J690*

These belt hooks complete our selection of ornamental jades for the warrior's equipment. Like their bronze counterparts (see, for instance *A.B.C. Bronzes*, Pls. LI and LII) most jade belt hooks consist of a body terminating in a hook on one end and of a short-shanked button located on the back of the other end. This button could be inserted into a button hole or into a slit in a strap or belt, while the hook was connected to a loop which could also be made of jade. As well exemplified here, hooks frequently took the shape of the heads of real or imaginary animals. It is interesting to note, incidentally, that the head of a nondescript monster which serves as the hook of the upper right belt-hook is very similar to those that decorate the shoulder of a gilt bronze lion in the Collection (cf. *A.B.C. Bronzes*, Pl. LIII, fig. A).[1] This head is completely reversible and can be read both ways, so that the cranial protuberance becomes a pointed beard. A flattened, contorted and dislocated animal with a bovine head forms the rest of this unusual item.

The body of the belt-hook with a feline head and an openwork spiralled wing-like excrescence is incised with compound C-shaped motifs. That of the belt hook with a dragon's head[2] is divided into three rectangular fields with designs in low relief, a floral design in the central field and conventionalized dragon heads on either side.

Similar dragon heads are incised on the rather thick edges of the buckle.

Published: B62 J40: Umehara, *Shina Ko-gyoku Zuroku*, Pl. LXXXIV; B60 J690: Loo, *Chinese Archaic Jades*, Pl. LVII, fig. 6

(1) See also Jenyns and Watson, *Chinese Art, The Minor Arts*, Pl. 8 for other variants of the same reversible head.
(2) Compare with a similar object found in 1972 in a tomb dating from the 3rd century B.C. and located at Pei-ling-sung shan, Chao-ch'ing city, Kuangtung (see *Wen Wu* 1974, no. 11, p. 76, fig. 26).

PLATE XVII

OVAL TUBE, Possibly a Hair Ornament

Light green with brown markings
Warring States or Western Han period (5th–1st century B.C.)
H. 6 in. *B60 J226*

SHELL-SHAPED ARTIFACT WITH A CENTRAL PERFORA-
TION, Possibly a Hair Ornament

Bluish grey with black markings
Warring States or Western Han period (5th–1st century B.C.)
L. 3 3/4 in. *B60 J609*

Here are two examples of a small group of objects which have not been properly identified in spite of the fact that they must have fulfilled some very specific functions.[1] They are characterized by relatively large dimensions, smooth asymmetrical contours and a total absence of decorative motifs. This last feature is strikingly unexcepted for a period which is best known for its ebullient over-all decoration. One of the charms of unostentatious objects of this type is that they fully enhance the visual and tactile qualities of the stone itself.

(1) According to one theory the oval tubes would have served to measure sacrificial grain; according to another, they were made in pairs to be used as ceremonial cuffs.

PLATE **XVIII**

STANDING FEMALE BEAR

Light grey-green with brown markings
Western Han period (2nd -1st century B.C.*)*
H. 4 1/8 in.   *B69 J57*

The animal stands on its hind legs, holds its head turned sideways and scratches its left ear. The posture and general appearance suggest a human caricature. The wrinkled face and the flaccid breasts give an indication of age which is rather rare for the period.

The animal has almost no neck, the muzzle is blunt and the open mouth shows two pairs of fangs—one pair up front and the other one at the rounded corners of the mouth, and a sharp tongue raised against the palate. The eyes are oval and are topped by thick spiralling eyebrows. The large ears are of the "spiral-and-point" type. A four-tufted striated mane is spread over the nape, the left shoulder and part of the back. It also covers part of the bifid horn which lies flat on the back. The tail is short, pointed and slightly twisted.

The forelegs are long and powerful when the back legs are short and have pointed tufts of hair back of the knees. The fingers of both "hands" and "feet" are abnormally long. Each comprises four clearly delineated phalanxes.[1]

The shoulders and haunches are decorated with spiral stems which are described as stylized wings by some authors. These convolutions play an important role as dating criteria. They first appear during the Han period as conventionalized variants of wing patterns and gradually evolve to the point where they look more like cloud or flame motifs. The entire mutation was apparently completed by the end of the Early Medieval period.[2]

Published: Gump, *Jade, Stone of Heaven,* p.199

(1) This, so far, unique piece closely resembles, stylistically as well as iconographically, two bronze feet discovered in 1968 in the tomb of Princess Tou Wan at Man-ch'eng, Hopei (See *The Exhibition of Archaeological Finds of the People's Republic of China, San Francisco catalogue*, nos. 166 and 167).

(2) See Pls. **XXIX, XXXIII** and **XXXVII.**

PLATE XIX

PENDANTS IN THE SHAPE OF HUMAN FIGURINES

Han period (2nd century B.C.*-2nd century* A.D.*)*

OPENWORK PENDANT, TORSO OF A DANCER   *(lower right)*
Ivory color, calcified
Western Han period (3rd-2nd century B.C.*)*
H. 1 1/8 in.   B60 J766
PENDANT IN THE SHAPE OF A MAN   *(lower center)*
Ivory color, calcified
H. 15/16 in.   B60 J593
PENDANT IN THE SHAPE OF A BEARDED MAN   *(lower left)*
Light green with white markings
H. 3/4 in.   B60 J580
PENDANT IN THE SHAPE OF A STANDING OFFICIAL .   *(upper right)*
Translucent off-white
Han period (2nd century B.C.*-2nd century* A.D.*)*
H. 1 1/8 in.   B60 J729
PENDANT IN SHAPE OF TWIN HUMAN FIGURES   *(upper left)*
Greenish white
H. 2 1/16 in.   B60 J638

In Chinese art human representations are rare prior to the Warring States. Starting from the 5th century B.C., however, man begins to assume an important position which will become a prominent one by Han times. The objects shown here and on the following plate illustrate the stylistic changes during the Han period. The earliest object, i.e. the openwork pendant, shows a vivid contrast between the plainness of the mask and the complexity of the bust as well as of the distorted arms which are covered with geometric patterns.[1] The openwork is bold. The contours are convulsive and, in their agitated manner, quite in keeping with the conflicting motifs of the garment. By contrast the other pendants have relatively simple and flowing contours which, however, does not exclude the first manifestations of motion as in the case of the Standing Official and the Twins or of three-dimensionality as in the case of the Small Men and also the Standing Official. The surface treatment, also, is reduced to a minimum; just a few shallow incisions to suggest facial features, collars, sleeves, belts or occasionally a symbol of rank like the perforated disc (*pi*) which hangs from the belt of the Standing Official. Incidentally, this unique, and so far unpublished, object sheds some new light on the problem of the utilization and significance of the *pi* in Han times and possibly earlier. With the exception of the Twins, all these pendants are with a vertical hole that runs from vertex to base.

Published: Salmony, *Chinese Jade,* Pl. XXI: 2; d'Argencé, *A.B.C. Chinese Treasures,* fig.41

[1] In 1973 a Western Han tomb located in the western suburbs of Nan-ch'ang, Chiangsi province, yielded a similar pendant but this one is full-length and made of ivory (See *K'ao Ku Hsiieh Pao* 1976, no. 2, Pl. 6, fig. 2). See also *Wen Wu* 1973, no.4, p. 24, fig. 8, nòs. 7, 8, and 9 for comparable jade pieces of the mid-Western Han period.

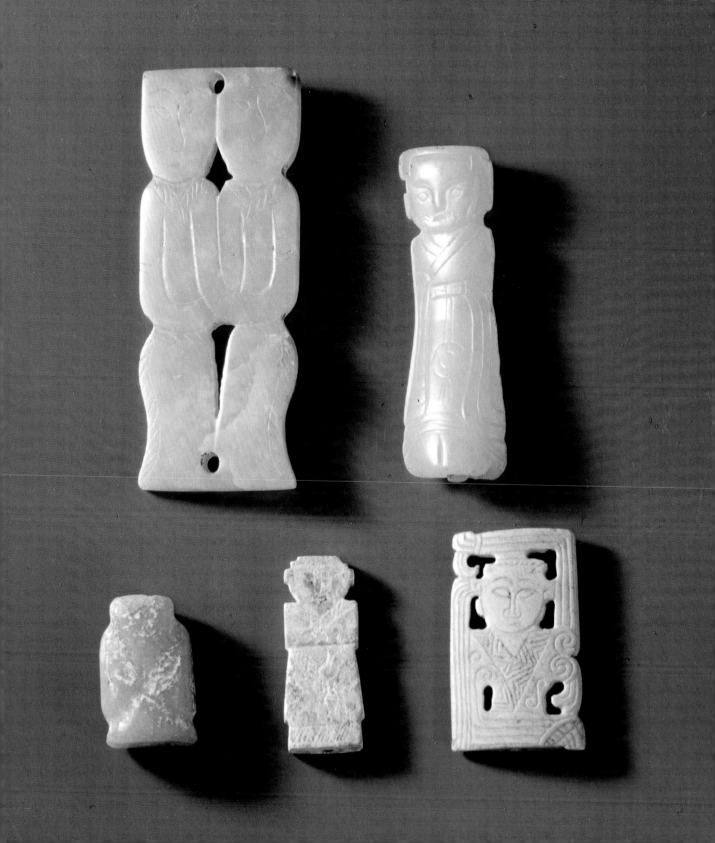

Plate XX

PENDANT IN SHAPE OF A BEARDED MAN

Yellowish green with brown and white markings
Han period (2nd century B.C.*-2nd century* A.D.*)*
H. 3 1/4 in.   *B60 J701*

Unlike Han potters who produced massive quantities of "human *ming-ch'i*" that portrayed all kinds of social types in the most varied occupations and states of mind, Han jade carvers seem to have restricted themselves to a few "aristocratic" series. In all likelihood, this is due to the fact that jade carvers were working for a few select mortals when the makers of clay figurines were working for the dead—all the dead, select or not.

Bearded men of this type probably constitute the largest group of human figurines of the Han period. They are characterized by elongated and almost featureless faces ending in disproportionately long beards and surmounted by flat or stepped hats. Bodies, treated geometrically, can be very compact and shortened to the point of appearing legless. Arms and hands are hidden under ample wing-like sleeves.

The present object is remarkable for its size and the quality of its workmanship. More than any other comparable pendant, it conveys a feeling of humoristic restraint. It is perforated with three convergent holes, one starting from the top of the head and the other two from behind the sleeves.

PLATE XXI

PI

Mottled green altered in parts
Han period (2nd century B.C.*-2nd century* A.D.*)*
Diam. 8 5/16 in.   *B60 J156*

More ancient perforated discs of large dimension were noted for a complete absence of surface decoration (cf. Pl. II). Here both sides are divided into two concentric zones in a manner which recalls the ornamental scheme of a number of contemporaneous bronze mirrors.

 The outer zone is decorated with four identical bovine masks in axial positions. To each head is attached a mane which bifurcates into symmetrical meanders, interrupted by conventionalized animal shapes. Long whiskers are indicated in very fine incisions; so are all other details including the criss-crossed circles and triangles behind the horns and at the base of the mane. Comparable arrangements are frequently seen on bronze vessels of Li-yü style.

 The inner zone consists of a regular hexagonal grain pattern in fairly high relief. Each grain is animated by an incised spiral and enclosed in a triangular setting of depressed lines which are nothing but tool marks. This zone is bordered by an outer and an inner incised rope band.[1]

Published: Huang Chün, *Ku Yü T'u Lu Ch'u Chi,* Peking,1939, vol. 1, Pl. 33; Loo,*Chinese Archaic Jades,* Pl. XXXVIII, fig.3; *d'Argencé, Propyläen,* Pl. 26

(1) A number of similar pieces, all ascribed to the Han period,have been discovered in recent years (See *Wen Wu* 1972, no. 5, p. 44, fig. 10, 1973, no. 4, p. 25, fig. 10 and p. 33, fig. 37, no. 3, 1976, no. 7, p. 57, fig. 1, no. 2; *K'ao Ku Hsüeh Pao* 1976, no. 2, p. 167,fig. 22, no. 2).

PLATE XXII

RECUMBENT BUFFALO

Mottled green with black and brown markings
Han period (2nd century B.C.*-2nd century* A.D.*)*
L. 7 3/8 in.   *B60 J18+*

Judging by the relatively large number of existing specimens, Han lapidaries and their affluent clientele were partial to small and occasionally medium sized animal figurines in the round. Numerically speaking, these animals form the most important group of the period.

Han animals can also be used as the best illustrations of the esthetic and technical revolution which took place shortly after the downfall of the Chou dynasty. The flat and heavily incised silhouettes of the Warring States are almost completely discarded and replaced by rounded volumes where even the few geometric patterns, which lingered on for a while, play a functional part. Animals are now studied from life and often endowed with individualized facial features. This is the advent of a new era which will even survive the Sung and Ch'ing antiquarian counter-revolutions.

This well-published and well-travelled buffalo also sheds some light on another significant aspect of the Han revolution: its thematic aspect. Han carvers opened up their vision by adding to the mythical beasts of former times all kinds of living species including domesticated animals and insects.

Published: Salmony, *Chinese Jade,* Pl. XXXVI; d'Argencé, *Apollo,* fig. 2 and *A.B.C. Chinese Treasures,* fig. 43; Rawson and Ayers, *Chinese Jade,* no. 241

PLATE XXIII

PENDANT IN THE SHAPE OF A BULL'S HEAD
White with brown markings
Warring States or Western Han period (5th-1st century B.C.*)* B60 J765
H. 1 in.

PENDANT IN THE SHAPE OF A TORTOISE
Mottled green with brown markings
Han period (2nd century B.C.*-2nd century* A.D.*)* B60 J703
L. 2 1/8 in.

CICADA
Light green
Eastern Han period (1st-2nd century A.D.*)*
L. 2 1/2 in. B60 J583

In their own peculiar manner, all three animals are good examples of the "conventionalized" naturalism which characterizes the Han approach. As stated elsewhere[1] Han artists could be surprisingly realistic without ever aiming at verisimilitude. They concentrated on the essential features of their subjects and overlooked all unnecessary details. In their attempts to capture the "bovineness" of their cattle, the "doggishness" of their dogs, the "reptileness" of tortoises, or the "insectness" of cicadas they sometimes produced more or less caricatural and humorous types, which somehow look more real than their models.

This attitude is not entirely new. Some of its aspects can be traced back at least as far as the Western Chou period (See Pl. IX).

Cicadas deserve a special mention as they were placed in the mouths of the dead where they served as tongue amulets. Such cicadas have been found in Han tombs in association with other pieces of jades used to close the apertures of the body.[2] In those days it was a common belief that jade and gold would preserve the body from putrefaction and the cicada itself was a symbol of cyclical resurrection.

Published: B60 J765: d'Argencé, *A.B.C. Chinese Treasures*, fig. 42. Compare also Jenyns, *Chinese Art, The Minor Arts II*, Pl. 151; B60 J703: Loo, *Chinese Archaic Jades*, Pl. XXX-1

(1) d'Argencé, *A.B.C. Ceramics*, p. 32

(2) See *K'ao Ku Hsüeh Pao* 1964, no. 2, p.127, fig. 22, no. 2 and *K'ao Ku T'ung Hsün* 1958, no. 9, p. 68, fig. 1 for an early Six Dynasties specimen.

PLATE XXIV

FINIALS IN THE SHAPE OF BIRDS

Late Han or Early Medieval period (2nd–6th century A.D.*)*

TOP, mottled tan with brown and black markings
L. 3 3/4 in.   *B60 J344*
BOTTOM, mottled black with white markings
L. 3 in.   *B60 J341*

The lower part of this plate shows, for the first time in photographic reproduction, a black and white dove which has intrigued specialists for nearly three-quarters of a century. Part of Wu Ta-ch'eng's collection, it was published in line-drawing by this eminent archeologist and pioneer of jadeology as early as 1889.[1] Several authors have since utilized Wu Ta-ch'eng's line-drawing when discussing the subject of Han birds, but the object itself had, for all practical purposes, disappeared from the scene until we rediscovered it on our shelves a few years ago.

One of the reasons why this invisible dove had become so famous is that jade birds that can be ascribed to the Han period are extremely rare.

These two examples share many common points. Shown in full profile and looking very alert they rest on a tubular base made for the insertion of a short shaft.[2] Heads have depressed eyesockets with sharp rounded pupils and terminate with slit beaks. Wings are tripartite. Shoulders are not feathered but instead are decorated with various geometric motifs, C-and-S-shaped spirals as well as circles and triangles for the dove, spiralling scrolls for the other bird.

In addition the dove presents three individual characteristics, a flattened crest, two hairy comma-shaped appendices on either side of the head and four attachment rings—two on the breast and two below the tail. The outstanding peculiarities of the other bird, obviously a pet, rest with its voluminous four-ridged tail and its elaborate necklace which is equipped with a small bell. The legs of this pet are tucked up and rendered rather casually in low relief while those of the dove are not indicated.

(1) Wu Ta-ch'eng, *Ku Yü T'u K'ao*, 1889, vol. 4, p. 129
(2) In the chapter dealing with ceremonies in his *History of the Later Han Dynasty* (*Hou-Han-shu Li-i-chih*) Fan Yeh tells us that each year in mid autumn those who had reached the age of eighty were presented with a foot long jade staff adorned at one end with the figure of a dove. The dove was chosen as the ideal gift for elderly persons because it is known for its ability to swallow and digest anything without choking and, of course, the gift implied that the recipient would perform likewise.

PLATE **XXV**

HORNED BEAR CARYATID
Mottled yellowish-green with brown markings
Late Han to Early Medieval period (1st-4th century A.D.*)*
H. 2 3/4 in.   *B65 J2*

CROUCHING PIG
Mottled brown with black markings
Early Medieval period (3rd-6th century A.D.*)*
L. 3 5/8 in.   *B65 J3*

The bear is a transitional piece in the sense that it retains a good deal of the Han approach, as we have just described it, while heralding the realistic trend which is going to prevail for several centuries until well into the Mid Medieval period.

Since Shang times the bear was one of the favorite themes of Chinese artists and craftsmen. It may be that it served as a link between the world of man and the animal kingdom on account of his quasi-human features and attitudes. By Han times the bear is the wild animal most frequently represented in bronze and pottery. Quite often Han bears serve as support for low tables or other pieces of furniture, or again, as pillar-bases for miniature houses. The shallow cylinder which rests on the neck of this rare jade example indicates that it must have fulfilled some comparable function. This animal, however, is a far cry from the usual statically squatting and hornless bear. It growls and gesticulates in the most menacing way. The presence of large, striated goat's horns on its head is another example of the typically Chinese relish for beasts made of components borrowed from various animals.

The sense of vitality that emanates from the pig is admittedly of a different order. All that is left of the Han approach is the posture, which shows the animal squatting and in full profile. Here there is no discrepancy between the treatment of the tense facial expression and that of the very expressive body which is itself so tense in its roundness that the animal seems to be resting on its belly rather than on its legs. All components flow smoothly into one another and contribute equally to the unmistakable "piggishness" of this pig. The contours, the mode of carving and the surface "crackling" suggest that this piece was fashioned from a pebble and buried over a long period of time.[1]

Published: B65 J2: A. Salmony, "A Chinese Jade Bear of the Early Han Period," *Artibus Asiae*, Vol. X/4, 1947, pp. 257-265; d'Argencé, *Apollo*, p. 135, fig. 2 (a); Rawson and Ayers, *Chinese Jade*, no. 191; B65 J3: d'Argencé, *Apollo*, p. 136, fig. 3 (a) and *A.B.C. Chinese Treasures*, p. 56, fig. 45; Rawson and Ayers, *Chinese Jade*, no. 199
(1) See *K'ao Ku* 1974, no. 6, Pl. 9, fig. 3 for two Chin dynasty stone specimens.

PLATE XXVI

FOUR ZOOMORPHIC PENDANTS

OTTER or SEAL   (*right*)
Blackish brown
Early Medieval period (3rd-6th century A.D.)
L. 5/8 in.   *B60 J898*
GOAT or IBEX   (*left*)
Greyish black
Early Medieval period (3rd-6th century A.D.)
L. 1 3/8 in.   *B60 J893*
RABBIT   (*bottom right*)
Light green with tan markings, altered in part
Early to Mid Medieval period (6th-10th century A.D.)
L. 1 1/4 in.   *B60 J368*
RODENT (Probably a squirrel)   (*bottom left*)
Tan with brown markings
Early to Mid Medieval period (6th-10th century A.D.)
L. 5/8 in.   *B60 J899*

The least refined, but also the most spirited, item in this group of small animals in the round is the otter or seal.   It may also be the oldest object in the group.   The very large head and the owlish eyes, crudely but convincingly carved, certainly point to an early dating.

All four figurines have many common characteristics: their diminutive sizes, their postures, a feeling of alertness, which can now be observed in the bodies as well as in the heads, and the absence of surface decoration with the exception of a few incisions which are essentially structural.

There is little doubt that such pendants were essentially used as trinkets in pretty much the same manner as those which were already fashionable some fourteen centuries earlier (cf. Pl. IX).

Published: B60 J368: Rawson and Ayers, *Chinese Jade*, no. 200

PLATE XXVII

SQUATTING MONSTER

Mottled brown with black markings
Early Medieval period (3rd–6th century A.D.*)*
H. 2 1/4 in.   *B65 J34*

So far as jade is concerned, the main contribution of the Early Medieval period may well consist of a large group of strange creatures in the round, of which this squatting monster is a good example.[1] Misshapen, hump-backed and crooked, these chimerae, winged lions, winged tigers, winged toads and many other nondescript animals with their gnarled features and awkward postures seem to be the products of half-scared, half-amused imaginations. They reflect a sort of morbid humour which may have been one of the characteristic traits of the literati in those days of turbulence and incertitude.

Many features of this monster recall those already observed in connection with the bear of Pl. XXV. Its body might, in fact, be that of a bear but it is surmounted by the head of a horned and bearded toad. The breasts and navel are suggested by nailmarks of a type which became extinct early in the Medieval period. The monster holds a rattle in its right forepaw and prayer beads in the left one, which gives one to think that it was conceived of as the caricature of a monk.

Published: d'Argencé, *A.B.C. Chinese Treasures*, p. 56, fig. 44

MONK'S HEAD

Grey green with brown markings
Early Medieval period (5th–6th century A.D.*)*
H. 1 3/8 in.   *B60 J782*

This pitted, jovial, almost roguish, head was probably part of a composite figurine, the rest of which may have been made of a different material. It reflects esthetic concepts which were widely accepted only after Buddhism was firmly implanted in China. The curved mouth and the deep groove on the upper lip are characteristic of Six Dynasties portrayals. The squinting eyes add a touch of eccentricity which is often associated with Ch'an (Zen) representations.

Published: Salmony, *Chinese Jade,* Pl. XLVI, fig. 2 (with erroneous provenance); Rawson and Ayers, *Chinese Jade,* no. 210

PLATE XXVIII

RECUMBENT LEONINE UNICORN (upper)

Light green with brown markings
Early Medieval period (3rd-6th century A.D.*)*
L. 5 1/4 in.   B62 J10

RECUMBENT FELINE UNICORN (lower)

Grey-green with yellow and brown markings
Early Medieval period (3rd-6th century A.D.*)*
L. 3 3/4 in.   B60 J450

There is frequently something helpless and pathetic about the ungainly beasts which form the bulk of the menagerie of the Early Medieval period. Although so far no textual or archeological evidence is known to support this hypothesis, one is tempted to think that they were made to serve as auspicious pets or fondlings for scholars. They also seem to translate in plastic terms some of the most imaginative and fantastic visions of ancient mythology.

These two beasts have a great deal in common.[1] Their reclining bodies are partly curled up and they lift up their left forepaw as if to hold or catch some object that could have been carved independently and could be the prototype of the brocaded ball associated with Buddhist lions of later times.[2] The heads of both animals are turned sideways. Bulky and trapezoidal, they end in blunt muzzles with mouths that stretch out widely. Bead-like and close-set eyes are bordered by bulging eyebrows with bumpy sides. Nail marks were carved on the ears, nose and tail of the larger animal and on the breast, neck, forehead and cheeks of the smaller one. Both also have their outer flank deeply ribbed.

These animals also differ in a number of details. The horn of the larger one bifurcates into two spirals and rests flatly on the neck and mane. Its tail is treated in the same manner with two spiralling branches. Each of these branches bears a central groove that runs lengthwise and a series of parallel nail marks running crosswise, a pattern whose origin goes back to the Warring States period (see for instance Pl. XII). The spine of the same animal is marked by pronounced undulations separated by deep grooves. On one side of this spine incised and pointed tufts of hair run from the tip of the mane to the tail like so many saw teeth.

This last feature is totally absent from the other animal whose spine is more simply marked by a deep sinuous groove and bifurcates at the end into a high relief spiral and a long, sinuous and striated tail. Its horn, too, ends in a spiral and is marked by a central incision but does not bifurcate. Furthermore, all visible articulations are underlined by bold spirals in high relief.

Published: B60 J450: Rawson and Ayers, *Chinese Jade*, no. 181

(1) Not only between themselves but also with our Standing Female Bear of Pl. XVIII which is ascribed to the Western Han. Future excavations may prove that the present dating of such pieces is much too conservative.

(2) See for instance Pl. LXXIX.

PLATE XXIX

WATER VESSEL IN THE SHAPE OF A CROUCHING UNICORN WITH FELINE BODY

Green with russet markings
Later part of Early Medieval period (ca. 6th century A.D.*)*
L. 4 1/2 in.   B60 J350

This animal belongs to a well known group which has almost unanimously been ascribed to the Wei period. [1]   On the other hand, it differs from most other comparable specimens by a head and limbs that are geometrized to the extreme.   The head is flat and trapezoidal, the mouth rectangular, the nose conical, the eyes oval, the ears cylindrical and the legs are built from an assemblage of circles and cones. All this seems to be the logical result of a trend which became manifest early in the Han period (see for instance Pl. XVIII).

The bold spiral stems which decorate the haunches (where they appear in relief) and the belly (where they are incised) may be conventionalized wings or flames or clouds.   They constitute one of the outstanding characteristics of this group of zoomorphs.[2]   The bushy, tripartite tail with striated tufts curves up and lies flat on the rump like that of a Keeshond.   Nail marks appear on the jaws, at the base of the horn, on the outer flank and the underside of the paws.   The body was hollowed out to form a receptacle, the circular opening in the middle of the back has lost its stopper.

(1)   Cf. for instance, Salmony, *Chinese Jade*, Pl. XLII and ff; Gure, *Selected Examples*, Pls. 13 and 18; Hansford, *Chinese Carved Jade*, Pls. 66 and 67.
(2)   See Salmony, *op. cit.*, same plates.

WATER VESSEL IN THE SHAPE OF A FANTASTIC ANIMAL PART BOVINE PART FELINE

Green with white specks and brown markings
Early to Mid Medieval period (6th–10th century A.D.*)*
L. 4 1/4 in.   B60 J353

This other water vessel is made of a short and stout tubular body, four identical "boneless" legs, a large bushy tail and a bulky bovine head with no neck to speak of. The nose, carved in very high relief, has a sunken and indented bridge and spiralling nostrils.   The bead-like eyes with incised pupils are set in conical sockets, the eyebrows are striated.   Two, "soft", two-pointed antlers rest on the top of the head on either side of a shallow cupola-shaped cranial protuberance.   The leaf-like ears are carved in high relief and the underside of the neck bears three deep undulating grooves suggesting creases in the hide.   The tail curls up and separates into four striated tufts which stem from an intricate network of small spirals.   The main articulations are marked by small spirals and the flanks by large nail marks. All four paws have five claws including one spur.   The circular opening in the middle of the back was carved in two steps.   The stopper, in the shape of a double gourd, is perforated with a small vertical hole.

PLATE XXX

CUP IN THE SHAPE OF A REGARDANT SWAN

Light green with brown markings
Early to Mid-Medieval period (6th–10th century A.D.)
L. 4 in.   B62 J12

The bird rests flatly on its folded legs.   Its wings half opened and its raised tail form three sides of an almost square receptacle.   The long neck is turned all the way back and the narrow, conical head rests on the fourth side.   The wings consist of three layers of feathers, two with chevronlike hatchings and the third one, in the region of the shoulder, with a pattern of plain scales.   The tail, spread out in seven different branches, has elongated feathers with an incised pattern of chevrons.

This bird recalls a few pottery receptacles of T'ang date.[1]

DOUBLE CYLINDRICAL VESSEL

Grey-green with brown markings
Mid to Late Medieval period (10th–13th century A.D.)
H. 3 1/2 in.   B60 J228

Such vases, sometimes known as "hero vases" or "victory cups", an adaptation of the Chinese term, *ying-hsiung p'ing* are said to have been trophies that were given to winners of sportive contests or military combats.   Usually they are carved all around, but for a small bridge at the top and bottom where they communicate by a small hole.   These illustrate the first wave of conscious archaism that occurred towards the later part of the Medieval period as a result of the publicity given to the works of Sung archaeologists in scholarly circles.   They seem to be supported on the back of a small cat-like animal whose main characteristic is a very long tail that bifurcates into two twisting branches.   On its head stands what may be a phoenix derivation with divergent crests shaped like a partly openwork scroll and projecting over the rim of the vases.   A heart-shaped motif is incised on the breast of this bird and the same motif appears on the belly, but this time in relief.[2]

On the other side of the vessel, an even more bizarre creature, which can be best described as bat-like, has a small feline head, wide spread C-shaped wings and an elongated body that ends in a bifid tail whose spiralling branches meet with the tail of the small animal of the base.   The decoration of the cups themselves borrows most of its details from the Warring States period.   Conversely, the lower zone displays a row of petals with a central depression and three vertical incisions, a feature which is usually recognized as an innovation of Sung jade decoration.[3]

Published: Rawson and Ayers, *Chinese Jade*, no. 321

(1)   Cf. Henry Trubner, *The Arts of the T'ang Dynasty*, Los Angeles, 1957, fig. 216
(2)   This motif is well attested in Warring States jades. See for instance, Umehara, *Kogyoku*, Pls. LXXXII, fig. 6 and LXXXIII, fig. 1.
(3)   See for instance Gure, *Selected Examples*, p. 156 (1 a,b) and Hansford, *Chinese Carved Jades*, Pl. 77.   Alfred Salmony would prefer an earlier dating as indicated in *Chinese Jade*, p. 235 and Pl. XXXXII, fig. 2.

PLATE XXXI

PHOENIX, probably a head ornament
Greyish green with iron rust and brown markings
Mid-Medieval period (7th–10th century A.D.)
H. 3 1/4 in.   *B65 J15*

The tense, yet graceful body, is so arched that one of the tail-feathers rests on the flattened crest. The legs compact, but with marked articulations, are joined together against the vertical side of the body. Rendered in fairly high relief, they are placed unnaturally close to the tail The beak, eyes and ears are incised in a manner that recalls those of the birds of Plate XXX.

The general movement is underlined by long sweeping incisions on the wing and tail. The wings consist of three layers of plain feathers without any detail to speak of and hardly any attempt was made to suggest feathers on the tail. Apparently, the craftsman was desirous to eliminate cumbersome, descriptive details that might have distracted from the sweeping movement and resorted almost exclusively to calligraphic effects.

There is a perforation on the underside and the bird is thought to have served as a head ornament.

Published: d'Argencé, *A.B.C. Chinese Treasures*, p. 58, Pl. 47

PLATE XXXII

CAMEL

Tan with brown veins
Mid-Medieval period (7th–10th century A.D.)
L. 3 1/4 in.   *B60 J869*

The camel made an ephemerous but spectacular passage in Chinese art. The vast majority of camel figures or figurines in any medium were made between the 6th and the 10th century, which was a time of intensive traffic along the desert avenues of Central Asia. Jade camels are exceedingly rare[1] and those that have been recorded seem to be in the same posture, reclining and biting their fore hump. This young animal is treated realistically but with a great economy of details. The surface decoration relies exclusively on the natural veins of the stone, on shallow striations to suggest the hair of the neck and humps and on simple incisions for eyes and nostrils. Conversely, the undersides of the feet were carefully modelled.

HORNED ELEPHANT

Grey-green with brown specks
Mid-Medieval period (7th–10th century A.D.)
L. 2 15/16 in.   *B60 J355*

One hesitates to speak of realism when describing a beast that is partly bovine, partly ovine and partly elephantine. Yet by the warm smoothness of the stone, the roundness of the contours, the built-in articulations, the watchful and tranquil posture and the almost complete absence of non-functional surface decoration, this hybrid belongs to the same plastic category with the camel, as opposed to the deformed creatures of the Early Medieval period.

The tip of the trunk is outlined by a kidney-shaped incision which, with two comma-shaped depressions for the nostrils, suggests the head of the *ling-chih*.[2] The ridge of the trunk is marked by a series of shallow indentations. The mouth, closed, is made of a deep groove bordered by lips in raised line. The small, bulging bead-like eyes are set in cone-shaped sockets with elongated outer canthi. They are brought together to the point where the animal is actually squinting which adds further to its mixed charms. The small, curved and torsated horns enclose the top of the head. The short, sturdy legs terminate in quadripartite cloven hooves of the ovine type. The crenelated spine ends in a bushy, striated tail equipped with a coiling secondary branch. The general appearance and the absence of tusks seem to indicate that this also is a young animal.

Published: d'Argencé, *Apollo*, p. 136, fig. 3 and *A.B.C. Chinese Treasures*, fig. 46 (different views)

(1)   A similar but more mature camel belongs to the Seattle Art Museum, Eugene Fuller Memorial Collection.

(2)   The *ling-chih*, a species of fungus, is considered by the Chinese as an emblem of longevity or immortality.

PLATE XXXIII

SQUATTING TWO-HORNED FELINE

Waxy greyish green with light to dark brown markings
Mid to Late Medieval period (8th–13th century A.D.)
L. 4 3/8 in.   *B60 J373*

It is always very tempting to try and match early mythical zoomorphs with names listed in ancient bestiaries. In most cases this is also a rather frustrating task as forms and descriptions rarely coincide. This animal, however, may be an exception. It has the head of a dragon on the body of a Buddhist lion, which corresponds to the definition of the *Pai-tsê*, an auspicious beast that was endowed with the gift of speech.

The head held straight and slightly raised has a blunt muzzle with an openwork mouth that reveals a small tongue and square teeth as well as two pairs of fangs. Flame-like tufts carved in low relief at the corners of the mouth constitute a new feature which may have evolved from the cheek wings of more ancient times.[1] The nose is triangular and deeply carved. The bead-like eyes are set in deep conical sockets. The enormous eyebrows are bushy and striated. The bifid mane rests on the back and is also striated. The two-pointed antlers curve down as they follow the contours of the mane. The jowls have a curious double outline and the short triangular goatee rests on a deeply grooved chest suggesting a row of overlapping scales. A copious, bushy and tripartite tail spreads over the rump and the back. The articulations at the shoulders are of the "spiral-and-point" type. All four paws have four claws with well carved undersides. Fine comb-like striations, mark the sides of the lower jaw and the outer sides of the legs.

Together with the flaming whiskers mentioned above the most distinctive features are the bold spirals which decorate the haunches and shoulders. The spiral stems on the shoulders are especially developed. The wings of the former periods are now reaching the last phase in the slow process of abstraction we have observed earlier (cf. Pl. XVIII) and look like flaming excrescences.

(1) See Gure, *Selected Examples*, Pl. 9, figs. 1a and 1b.

Plate XXXIV

RHYTON IN THE SHAPE OF A BULL'S HEAD[1]

Dark brown
Mid-Medieval period (7th–10th century A.D.*)*
H. 3 1/2 in.   *B60 J246*

Throughout the Medieval period, table ware and especially drinking vessels were produced in a variety of shapes reflecting, at times, vastly different tastes.

Boot-shaped cups and rhyta appeared for the first time as a result of consecutive waves of Central Asian and Near Eastern influence. Very few of these libation cups, which the 18th century antiquarians called by a variety of names, including *ch'iu,*[2] have been illustrated in scholarly publications, probably because they are rare in Western collections. Ours contains a dozen of them, of which the present object is the oldest and the most Western looking. It shows marked similarities with Iranian silver wares of the Sassanian period, particularly in the treatment of the eyes and eyebrows which look distinctly un-Chinese.[3] The pierced nostrils also serve as a suspension hole.

The jade was chosen and probably treated to imitate natural horn. The resemblance is striking.[4]

Published: Fontein and Wu, *Unearthing China's Past,* Boston,1973, p. 181, no. 94; Rawson and Ayers, *Chinese Jade,* no. 206

(1) See *Ku Yü T'u P'u,* ch. 90, 1a for the line-drawing of an almost identical rhyton.
(2) Cf. Pl. LIX.
(3) Cf. R. Ghirshman, *Artibus Asiae,* XXVI, 1, (1962), fig. 28.
(4) See *Wen-hua Ta Ko-ming Ch'i-chien Ch'u-t'u Wen-wu,* Peking,1972, Pl. 70 for a parallel in onyx dating from the T'ang dynasty.

PLATE XXXV

CUP AND BOWL

Greyish-green with brown and black markings
Mid to Late Medieval period (8th–13th century A.D.)
The Cup, B60 J467, is 4 3/8 in. high and the Bowl, B60 J221, is 3 5/8 in. in diameter

These rare objects offer a refreshing contrast with the usual jade containers attributable to the period in question.   One cannot help being fascinated by the simplicity of their contours and the plainness of their surfaces.   Both are made in imitation of prototypes in other materials.

The cup is derived from metallic models.   No attempt was made to conceal or even smooth away the sharp articulations where the foot and the handle meet with the body or the edges of the lip and shoulders, which all result from the soldering or beating of relatively soft metals such as silver.   This type of handle, with a flat flange and a knobbed loop, has parallels in silver wares of the Sung period[1].   The perfectly round depression on the side opposite to the handle does not quite make sense unless one accepts the idea that it was made to hide a flaw or a chip.

One of the ideals of the Chinese potters was to produce wares that would look like jade, a wish that came true with some Sung celadons.   Only rarely did early jade carvers pay them back in their own coin.   This bowl seems to be an exception.   The thickness of its walls, the robustness of its silhouette, the roundness of the mouth rim, all are reminiscent of certain types of Sung monochromes.   On the other hand, the peculiar foot-rim is more likely to be a derivation of metallic models.

Published: B60 J467: Rawson and Ayers, *Chinese Jade*, no. 273; B60 J221: Rawson and Ayers, *ibidem*, no. 268

(1)   Cf. *T.O.C.S.*, vol. 32, Pl. 18, fig. 35; Pl. 23, fig. 43; Pl. 63, no. 164.

PLATE XXXVI

CYLINDRICAL CUP WITH HANDLE

Grey-green with brown markings
Late Medieval period (10th–14th century A.D.)
H. 4 in.   *B60 J429*

At first glance, the main zone of decoration of this cup is difficult to decipher, owing to an unusual technical approach whereby the principal design appears not in relief but in intaglio against a slightly raised background of C-and-S-shaped spirals. This sunken design consists of a bird and a feline seen in profile and confronting each other. Each is treated fairly realistically with the exception of the tail. These geometric tails are unexpectedly large and frame the animals on three sides. They are provided with several outgrowths set at right angles with the right stem and in more than one way recall the wings of the "phoenix" of Plate XXX.

Both silhouettes are crested and bearded. Legs have two claws each and bear incised flame motifs or stylized wings. In each case, one leg is raised in what seems to be a menacing attitude and the whole arrangement looks like a heraldic combat scene.

The lip zone is incised with interlocked T-shaped meanders.

The large, heavy and angular handle displays on its flat top an incised pattern showing a buffalo head of a style comparable to those of the *pi* illustrated on Pl. XXI. Surmounting this head is a curious pattern made of two ear-like elements placed above an anchor-shaped spiral and between two heart shapes.

The upper parts of the three feet consist of miniature bovine heads, which resemble in a simplified way that of the handle.

There is some comb hatching on parts of the crests, legs and tails.

Many of the features that have just been described are of Warring States origin; others like the shape of the handle and its decoration or again the lip zone decor and a few compound spirals on the bodies of the animals are anachronic details, which point to a much later date. Alfred Salmony published a group of similar cups which he ascribed to the Wei period[1]. We prefer to retain a more conservative attribution[2] since all indications are that these cups were conscious recaptures of ancient models rather than the products of a dying tradition.

It would seem that in most cases these cups were made with lids but most lids have disappeared.

Published: d'Argencé, *Apollo*, p. 138, fig. 4 (b)

(1) Salmony, *Chinese Jade*, Pl. XXXVIII and XXXIX.

(2) See for instance *T.O.C.S.*, vol. 32, Pl. 91, fig. 264 and Gure, *Selected Examples*, Pl. 31, fig. 4.

PLATE XXXVII

RHYTON

Light green with brown markings
Late Medieval period (10th–14th century A.D.)
H. 6 1/4 in.   B60 J473

It did not take long for rhyta to become fully sinicized. This one, for instance, relatively early as it is, retains practically nothing of the Western influence that our plate XXXIV made so evident.

The cup looks like a truncated horn with irregular contours. A narrow border of square meanders encircle the mouth rim and the base is made of two inverted animal heads. One side shows a monster's mask with open jaws, spiralling nose and ears, horns, that are carved in high relief and a rounded forehead that is incised with an inverted heart shape.[1] The other side shows the suggestion of an elephant's head with a spiralling trunk. These heads are fully integrated since the ears of the monster are also the eyes of the elephant.

An almost free-sculptured dragon climbs along one side of the vessel with its head resting over the rim. It probably served as a handle. This lean and lithe creature with its blunt muzzle, its triangular face that widens emphatically in the region of the cheeks and brows, its prominent ears, its single spiralling horn that rests limply on a bushy striated mane and its sweeping tail that bifurcates into two coiling branches belongs to a category of dragons which is well attested in art since the Warring States period (see for instance the scabbard buckle of Pl. XIV). It was known as a hydra earlier in the century. The Chinese call it *ch'ih* and a Ming zoologist described it as an "immature dragon".[2] The spine of this one is made of sharp tooth-like projections. It has spiralling articulations, stylized "wings" on thighs and shoulders. Its ribs are indicated by a series of eight parallel incisions and its powerful claws are clearly delineated. Two other frolicking *ch'ih* with dislocated bodies but otherwise similar features are carved in fairly high relief on the body of the vessel. Apparently, they are engaged in a celestial game of hide and seek against a background of incised clouds.

The theme may not be altogether original[3] but the carving of this piece is unusually free and bold.

(1) Cf. with "victory cup" of Pl. XXX.
(2) See *Oriental Art*, New Series, vol. 2, no. 3, 1956, p. 100.
(3) For several other variants see *T.O.C.S.*, vol. 32, Pls. 88 and 89.

PLATE XXXVIII

CHIH-SHAPED CUP WITH RING HANDLE (right)

Grey-green with brown and black markings
Late Medieval period (11th–14th century A.D.*)*
H. 3 1/2 in.   *B60 J222*

TOU-SHAPED CUP WITH LID (left)

Off-white with brown and black markings
Late Medieval or Early Ming period (14th–16th century A.D.*)*
H. 5 3/4 in.   *B60 J245*

These vessels differ from the archaistic specimens we have discussed so far[1] in that they imitate not only Warring States features, but also Shang and Western Chou shapes and decorative motifs. This innovation was no doubt the result of discoveries of actual Shang and Western Chou bronzes, but there is no indication that in those days the jade carvers ever had a chance to study the bronze vessels at close range. On the contrary, their inaccurate and frequently clumsy rendering of shapes and details suggest that they worked from written descriptions or at best from line drawings.

In this sense these containers must be regarded as important landmarks and as forerunners of the better known 18th century group of archaistic vessels which are made essentially after Shang and Western Chou models.[2]

The *chih*-shaped cup[3] is decorated on the neck with a band of whorl-circles and confronting, gaping dragons in low relief against a background of incised square meanders. All these motifs are borrowed with some unexpected modifications from Late Shang or Early Western Chou bronze vessels. On the contrary the ring handle with its curved thumb-piece is similar to that of a famous Warring States casket which was found at Chin-ts'un, Honan[4]. Interestingly enough the same type of handles were current in metal work during the Sung dynasty[5].

In spite of its awkward silhouette, the other item, the *tou*, is a more straightforward imitation of an ancient bronze vessel. Here no foreign appendix was added. The receptacle is decorated with a large band of monsters' masks of the *t'ao-t'ieh* type. They appear in low relief against a background of criss-cross pattern. A large section of the lower part of the stem is filled with a rather coarse imitation of the classical square meanders. The only notable anachronism is the leaf border incised on the lid. This motif, however, is very revealing since it is a variation of a typical late Yüan or Early Ming ceramic pattern.[6]

Published: B60 J222: d'Argencé, *Apollo*, p. 138, fig. 4; B60 J245: Rawson and Ayers, *Chinese Jade*, no. 332
(1)   See for instance Pls. XXX and XXXVI.
(2)   See for instance Pls. LII, LIV, LVI, LVIII and LX.
(3)   See *A.B.C. Ancient Chinese Bronzes*, Pl. XVIII (B) for a similar shape of Shang date.
(4)   See Hansford, *Chinese Jade Carving*, Pl. XX, b.
(5)   See for instance *T.O.C.S.*, vol. 32, figs. 228 and 239, see also fig. 281 for another jade example.
(6)   See Jenyns, *Ming Pottery and Porcelain*, Pl. 19 for one of the earliest illustrations of the motif.

PLATE XXXIX

PERFORATED DISC WITH CH'IH-DRAGONS

Bluish-grey with tan markings, altered in parts
Late Medieval or Early Ming period (14th-16th century A.D.)
Diam. 5 1/2 in.   *B65 J7*

In jade carving few zoomorphs can claim a perennity equal to that of the young or "immature" dragon which the Chinese call *ch'ih*.   Few have been so often depicted in so many different aspects and in so many different ways.[1]

Here a perforated disc of the *pi*-type[2] serves as a playground for nine of these animals.   Seven of them look sufficiently alike to belong to the same litter.   As for the other two, one has a short snout and tusks and the other the head of a phoenix.   They all display features that are already well known to us[3] and will remain surprisingly consistant until well into the Ch'ing dynasty[4].   What distinguishes them from later specimens is above all the tautness of their attitudes. One feels that each muscle, each tendon is working to its maximum.   One should also note the very careful placing of these animals and the absence of environmental accessories.

(1)   See for instance Pls. XIV, XXXVII, XL and LVII.
(2)   See Pls. II, XV and XXI.
(3)   See Pl. XXXVII for a detailed description.
(4)   See for instance, Hansford, *Chinese Carved Jades*, Pl. 96.

PLATE XL

OVAL BASIN

Dark green with brown and black markings
Late Medieval or Early Ming period (14th–16th century A.D.)
L. 10 in.   *B60 J59*

This unusual basin may well have been inspired by such oversized wine vessels as the famous Yüan piece known as the "Black Jade Wine Bowl", which was rescued by Emperor Ch'ien-lung from a Taoist temple where it was used as a receptacle for vegetables.[1]

Elleptical in shape, thick-walled, much wider at the girth than at the lip and absolutely plain inside, it is covered on the outside with an ebullient pattern of what seems to be a variety of "dragons" amidst a background of curling clouds. The carving is unusually bold and deep and some elements of this close-knit composition are actually done in openwork. The dragons, five in number, are hornless. They have two-clawed paws, bifurcated tails and flame motifs or stylized wings on their shoulders and haunches. Otherwise, they all look different. Two have no mane and one of these has the head of a rat or a bat.[2]

Published: Gump, *Jade*, p. 161
(1) See Hansford, *Chinese Jade Carving*, p. 75 and Pl. XXVIIIa.
(2) See the preceding plates for other examples of dragons with heads of other animals.

PLATE XLI

WINE CUP. CHANG CH'IEN IN HIS HOLLOW LOG FLOATING DOWN THE YELLOW RIVER

Grey-green with brown and black markings
Late Medieval or Ming period (14th–17th century A.D.)
L. 4 1/4 in.   *B60 J162*

Chang Ch'ien, traveler, general and statesman of the Western Han dynasty, has passed into history as the Great Explorer.   Legend has it that he brought back wine from Central Asia as well as the method to make it.   Another legend, of southern origin, says that he went up to the source of the Yellow River and thence directly on to its celestial counterpart, the Milky Way.

The present cup seems to illustrate a synopsis of these themes.   Chang Ch'ien is shown sitting in what looks like a hollow vine-stock floating down the river. The rope that encircles one of the extremities of the log serves to secure a double gourd that is hanging on the other side and the back of the log is perforated with two suspension holes.

Cups of this type are known to exist in silver[1] and rhinoceros horn[2].   They range in dates from the middle of the fourteenth century to the Ch'ing period and the earlier ones (all made of silver) may have served as models for our jade cup which, incidentally, has no known counterpart.

This piece is different from everything we have seen so far, in view of its anecdotic character.   It heralds a new era which must have originated during the Yüan period or early during the Ming dynasty.   This is a major turning point in the history of Chinese jades.   From now on they will narrate and portray[3], as well as symbolize.   Narrations and portrayals will generally be inspired by famous episodes or personages of the Chinese history of folklore.   One of the most significant consequences of this new trend is that the individualized man, who was so conspicuously absent heretofore, will now become a familiar theme.   It must be noted that, in this respect at least, lapidaries showed considerable conservatism since in practically all other art forms man was already a central figure at a much earlier date.

Published: Rawson and Ayers, *Chinese Jade,* no. 357

(1)   viz. Sherman E. Lee and Wai-Kam Ho, *Chinese Art Under the Mongols: The Yüan Dynasty (1279–1368),* Cleveland, 1968, no. 37.
(2)   viz. Michel Beurdeley, *L'Amateur Chinois,* Fribourg, 1966, cat. 58.
(3)   Cf. Pls. XLII, XLIV, LXI, LXIV, LXV, LXVI, LXVII and LXXIII.

PLATE XLII

THREE BOYS PLAYING WITH A LARGE JAR

Mottled greenish-grey with brown markings
Early Ming period (16th century A.D.)
H. 3 1/4 in.   B60 J164

Three small boys, one holding a lotus stem, another one holding a *ju–i* sceptre,[1] and the third one with a *sheng*, a musical instrument made of bamboo pipes of different lengths, are trying to climb on top of a big jar.   The carving is unusually strong and lively but not altogether exempt of mannerisms.   For instance, the attitudes of the children are somewhat affected and they all keep their eyes tightly closed for no apparent reason.[2]

The jar is decorated in low relief with a border of *ju–i* lappets[3] around the mouth rim and petal panels around the foot.   This type of decoration[4] and the shape of the jar[5] point to a mid-16th century date corresponding to the Chia-ching period (1522–1566).   Furthermore, children at play were a common motif of decoration for blue-and-white and enamelled porcelains of the period in question.   This is, consequently, one of the rare cases when one is tempted to narrow an attribution down to a specific reign mark in the Ming dynasty.

(1) See Pl. LXXIX
(2) This may well be one of the earliest examples in the collection of the complex rebuses that became so commonplace during the Ming and Ch'ing dynasties (Cf. for instance Pls. XLVIII, LXI and LXXVIII). This one has not been properly identified, but a tentative interpretation would imply a wish to an official for rapid promotion.
(3) So called because they resemble the heads of *ju–i* sceptres.   They also recall a heart-shaped motif of Warring States origin, Cf. Pl. XXX [note (2)]
(4) See for instance, Jenyns, *Ming Pottery and Porcelain*, Pl. 90 B and Garner, *Oriental Blue and White*, Pls. 50 and 51.
(5) See Cornelius Osgood, *Blue-and-White Chinese Porcelain, a Study of Form*, New York, 1956, pp. 119–120.

PLATE XLIII

RECLINING HORNLESS ANTELOPE

Grey-green with brown markings
Late Medieval or Ming period (14th-17th century A.D.)
H. 3 1/8 in.   *B64 J3*

The animal is recumbent but one of the forelegs is half raised and stands vertically against the body in a posture which appears to be an innovation of the period in question. The head, very large and slightly raised, is turned all the way back. With its arched forehead and nose, it resembles that of a camel. The jaws are strongly marked, the ears are large and pointed. The slightly protuberant eyes are almond-shaped. The top of the head is covered with spiraling leaves or fungi in lieu of antlers. The center of the undersides of the cloven hooves are marked with two semicircular depressions. The short tail ends in a striated tuft. All articulations are plain and well delineated. The animal holds in its mouth a branch of *ling-chih* fungus, the extremities of which rest on the back and sides. The symbolic message is quite clear since both the deer and the *ling-chih* are emblems of longevity and, indeed, the deer "is said to be the only animal to find the sacred fungus"[1].

ELEPHANT

Grey-green with brown markings
Ming or Early Ch'ing period (15th-17th century A.D.)
L. 3 1/4 in.   *B60 J363*

Practically all the animals discussed so far were reclining, crouching or crawling. In fact, standing animals are extremely rare prior to the Ming dynasty. The passage from one posture to the other essentially reflects technical improvements accompanied by bolder experiments. Only very self-confident craftsmen would dare carve legs in the round. It is to be noticed that in early examples like this one the legs are short, thick and hardly separated from the body.

In contrast with the hybrid shown on Plate XXXII this is a real elephant and a very individualized one at that[2]. It is obviously a very old, almost decrepit animal, as can be seen from the deep creases over the hind legs. These irregular spiraling furrows are arranged in such a way that they suggest a sort of cloud motif. The head is held very low and turned almost all the way back. A short, curved trunk ends in a large flat nozzle. Two long pointed tusks project from the closed mouth, the corners of which are accentuated by a series of grooves suggesting wrinkles. The very long and wrinkled ears have deep central depressions. The stocky legs end in five-nailed feet, whose undersides are carved with great care.

In Buddhism such an elephant is regarded as one of the Seven Treasures[3]. In a broader context, "the elephant is the symbol of strength, sagacity and power."[4]

Published: B64 J3: Rawson and Ayers, *Chinese Jade,* no. 264

(1) Williams, *Outlines of Chinese Symbolism and Art Motives,* p. 116. (2) Cf. Gorer and Blacker, *Chinese Porcelain and Hard Stones,* vol. I, fig. 106. (3) Mayers, *The Chinese Reader's Manual,* p. 351, no. 228. See also *T.O.C.S.,* vol. 30, Pl. 94, fig. 357 for a comparable "Ming" example. (4) Williams, *op. cit.,* p. 170.

PLATE XLIV

MAN GROOMING A HORSE

Light green with brown markings
Ming period (14th–17th century A.D.)
L. 6 in.   B60 J388

STANDING HORSE WITH TWO MONKEYS

Grey-green with red and brown markings
Ming period (14th–17th century A.D.)
L. 4 5/8 in.   B64 J5

Flat and roughly rectangular or oval bases were used at least as early as the Western Han to support standing quadrupeds,[1] but apparently Ming carvers were the first to sculpt these slabs into natural landscape settings such as rocks, tree trunks, waves of the sea or rivers, etc. Modest as they are, such "landscapes" constitute a significant turning-point in the development of Chinese jade carving. They reflect a broader vision which now includes the whole of nature. In a way they can be regarded as the prototypes of the famous jade mountains of subsequent periods.[2]

The Chinese are great lovers of horses and this love finds many illustrations in Chinese art as early as the Shang dynasty.[3] Jade horses, however, are very rare until after the Sung dynasty when the noble Bactrian horse, which T'ang potters have made world-famous, had all but disappeared from the Chinese soil to be replaced by the stocky Mongolian pony. We have here two big-bellied, short-legged, long-necked and long-tailed specimens of this hardy breed. The heads are massive and one of the foreheads is conspicuously arched, which for horses is a sign of stubbornness. Both groups are treated with a good deal of humor. The horse and groom, squatting as they are on their short, gnarled legs, seem to be in the throes of an irresistible fit of laughter.

Horses and monkeys are often shown together in carving of the Ming and Ch'ing periods. This is not merely a pleasant decorative arrangement. Monkeys were frequently kept in stables as their presence was supposed to protect the horses from all kinds of disease.[4] The large bee incised on the shoulder of this horse is not just an additional humoristic or realistic touch either. It plays an important part in a typical rebus which can be read as follows: "May you be soon elevated to the rank of marquis."[5]

Published: Gump, *Jade, Stone of Heaven*, p. 158; Rawson and Ayers, *Chinese Jade*, no. 366
(1) See *K'ao Ku* 1973, no. 3, Pl. XII illustrating a mounted horse ascribed to the late 3rd century B.C.
(2) See Pls. LXIV through LXVII.
(3) Cf. d'Argencé, *A.B.C. Bronzes*, Pl. XXV, A.
(4) See Williams, *Outlines*, p. 224 quoting the *Pen Ts'ao*, a Chinese Treatise on Medicine that was published in 1596.
(5) In colloquial Chinese "on horseback" (*ma shang*) also means "soon", "bee" (*feng*) is homonymous with "to be appointed" and "monkey" (*hou*) with "marquis". See also Pls. XLII, XLVIII, LXI, LXXI and LXXVIII.

PLATE XLV

DUCK WITH A BRANCH IN ITS BEAK

Off-white and tan
Ming period (14th–17th century A.D.)
L. 2 3/16 in.   *B60 J332*

FISH HOLDING LOTUS IN MOUTH

Off-white with brown markings
Ming period (14th–17th century A.D.)
L. 4 1/2 in.   *B60 J247*

The motif showing an animal holding a plant in its mouth or beak can be traced back to at least the T'ang dynasty,[1] but did not become very popular until much later. During the Ming period, when the motif was in great favor with jade carvers, it served to emphasize the streamlined contours of birds and fishes, as well quadrupeds. It was also used frequently as a subtle means of suggesting motion.

The head of the carp is flat, bulky and scaleless. The slanting mouth and the large oval eyes give to the face an expression of intensity. If fins and tail are depicted in some detail, the body proper is as plain as the head with the exception of a sweeping incision that runs longitudinally from gills to tail and a few incised three-branched stars. To our knowledge this last motif is a fairly late mannerism, which does not occur in Chinese art prior to the Ming dynasty.

Ming zoomorphs can be bulky and compact to the point of looking slightly distorted.[2] With its rounded contours and its small head leaning to one side, this duck is a case in point. It was probably carved out of a pebble and with great economy of means. Only the wings and the shoot of corn are rendered in some detail.

Both the fish and the bird rest on "bases" that suggest their natural environment.[3] They consist of whirlpools of finely incised waves. In the case of the fish the whirlpool expands on the sides and forms clawlike wavelets that are carved in fairly high relief.

(1) See for instance Trubner, *The Arts of the T'ang Dynasty*, p. 113, No. 305
(2) See also preceding plate
(3) See caption, preceding plate

PLATE XLVI

WATER RECEPTACLE IN SHAPE OF BUDDHA'S HAND (CITRON)
Grey-green with brown markings
Ming period (15th-17th century A.D.*)*
L. 8 in.   *B60 J9+*

The vegetable kingdom was not a main source of inspiration for jade carvers until late in the 18th century, with the exception of a few Warring States timid attempts,[1] and examples of plant carvings are practically nonexistant prior to the Ming dynasty, when they were almost entirely restricted to three subjects: the lotus, the Buddha's hand and the fungus, all three chosen for their symbolic value.

Exceptional as it is, this object serves as a vivid illustration of the Ming approach to jade carving. Unlike their predecessors Ming lapidaries relied almost exclusively on robust volumes and tactile surfaces. Unlike their successors they managed to hide their frequently astonishing virtuosity and to make it pass as a matter of course. Ch'ing carvers made tours de force, which were meant to be admired as such; not so with Ming carvers whose tours de force seem to be entirely natural. The tendrils, stem and leaves of this citrus medica are so deeply carved that they stand almost in the round. At the same time all these elements are architecturally integrated. This is the secret of a period when more than ever before or after jades were carved to be fondled as much as looked at.

This fruit is known as Buddha's hand because of a somewhat remote similarity between the position of its tendrils and that of Buddha's fingers in a few typical hand gestures. "It is also a symbol of wealth as it illustrates the gesture of grasping money."[2]

Published: Joan Hartman,*Chinese Jade of Five Centuries,* Pl.7; Rawson and Ayers, *Chinese Jade,* no. 355

(1)   See for instance Pl. XV.

(2)   Williams, *Outlines,* p. 51.

PLATE XLVII

TIGER AND THE FIVE POISONOUS ANIMALS

Grey-green with brown markings
Late Ming-Early Ch'ing period (ca. 17th century A.D.)
L. 4 1/4 in.   *B60 J352*

The tiger is sometimes included among the Five Poisonous Animals but in this context it plays the role of a mere, if ideal, vehicle for the animals in question. These are the viper, scorpion, centipede, toad, and spider. As a group they have the power to protect people and especially children from pernicious influences.

The tiger, sitting on its hind legs, bends affectionately over the toad as though the latter were its cub. It carries on its back and right side the spider, snake and centipede while the hornlike scorpion rests on the nape. The sides of the tiger's head, body and paws, are curiously flattened. The articulations are plain but the top of the forehead, as well as the haunches, sports "rotating hair whorls" of a type which apparently is not attested prior to the Ming dynasty.

RECUMBENT WATER BUFFALO AND CH'I-LIN CUB

Light green with brown markings
Late Ming-Early Ch'ing period (ca. 17th century A.D.)
H. 2 1/8 in.   *B60 J382*

This other unusual group illustrates one of the several legends according to which a *ch'i-lin* was born of a cow.[1] Such illustrations, whether in jade or in other materials, are exceedingly rare even though the *ch'i-lin* was generally regarded as a cross between either a dragon and a cow or a dragon and a deer.[2] Together with the dragon, the phoenix and the tortoise, the *ch'i-lin* is one of the four divine animals.[3] A creature of good omen, it symbolizes "longevity, grandeur, felicity, illustrious offspring and wise administration".[4] Its appearances were exceptional as they usually coincided with "the advent of good government or the birth of virtuous rulers."[5] It is quite possible that the present group was made as a gift to prospective parents, so they may be blessed with a talented son.

With its bulky proportions, its massive head and its flattened forehead and nose, the cow belongs to a relatively well-known group of oxen and buffaloes that are generally ascribed to the Ming or Transitional periods.[6] The right foreleg is typically half-raised and held close to the body.[7]

(1) Ball, *Decorative Motives of Oriental Art*, pp. 36–38
(2) *ibid.*, p. 33
(3) Williams, *Outlines of Chinese Symbolism and Art Motives*, p. 414. See also Pl. XLIX
(4) Williams, *op. cit.* p. 414.
(5) Mayers, *Manual*, p. 136
(6) See for instance *T.O.C.S.* vol. 30, Pl. 93; Hansford, *Chinese Carved Jades*, Pl. 84;
(7) Cf. Pl. XLIII

Plate XLVIII

FIVE BATS

Grey-green with brown markings
Late Ming-Early Ch'ing period (17th century A.D.)
W. 4 in.   *B60 J95*

The Chinese will never miss a chance to make puns and at times these puns become well established symbols and art motives.[1]   In the national language or mandarin the words bat and happiness are homonyms (*fu* in both cases).   This suffices to explain why the bat became emblematic of happiness.   By way of consequence five bats automatically symbolize the Five Blessings which are traditionally longevity, riches, peacefulness and serenity, love of virtue and natural death.   This group, which consists of two adults and three small ones all huddling together, may also be interpreted as a symbol of domestic happiness.

The carving has the structural robustness and the warm waxy surface usually associated with objects of the Ming period, but unlike typical Ming carvings it contains a good deal of abstraction.   The shapes are conventionalized and with the exception of a few comb-like hatchings to suggest hair, the surface details consist of sweeping double incisions and spirals, which are only vaguely functional. Their main purpose is to create a feeling of gyrating motion in a manner which, to be convincing, foreshadows the decorative devices of the Ch'ing period[2].

(1) See also Pls. XLII, XLIV, LXI, LXXI and LXXVIII
(2)   Cf. Donnelly, *The Animal in Chinese Art*, Pl. 11c

Plate XLIX

RHYTON WITH PHOENIX IN RELIEF

Grey-green with black and brown markings
Late Ming or Early Ch'ing period (ca. 17th century A.D.)
H. 10 1/8 in.   *B60 J472*

The cup is in the shape of a slightly curved and truncated horn. In contrast with earlier rhyta,[1] its base is not zoomorphic but generates a curious phoenix which is as much a plant as it is a bird. This vegetable gallinacean grows out of one side of the foot and creeps along the wall of the cup like some sort of tropical vine with spiraling outgrowths in lieu of crest and wings. The head only is easily recognizable and resembles those which Late Ming potters have made famous.[2] All joints, articulations and also occasionally terminals of the "crest" and "wing" are incised with small spirals that curl up very tightly. These spirals and the vegetable outgrowths permit us to place this object at the juncture of the Ming and Ch'ing dynasties.[3]

Together with the dragon, the unicorn and the tortoise, the phoenix is one of the four supernatural creatures. "It presides over the southern quadrant of the heavens and, therefore, symbolizes sun and warmth for summer and harvest."[4] "In poetry many covert allusions to sexual pairing are intimated by reference to the inseparable fellowship of the feng and the hwang"[5] which are respectively the male and female of this mythical species. The phoenix is also a symbol of beauty, peace and prosperity.[6]

Published: Gump, *Jade*, p. 152
(1) Cf. Pls. XXXIV and XXXVII.
(2) See Jenyns, *Ming Pottery and Porcelain*, Pl. 100 B.
(3) See Jenyns, *Later Chinese Porcelain*, Pl. XXXVI (1) and *Sekai Tōji Zenshū*, vol. 12, Pls. 46 and 47 for dragon handles treated in the same manner.
(4) Williams, *Outlines of Chinese Symbolism and Art Motives*, p. 325
(5) Mayers, *The Chinese Reader's Manual*, p. 43, no. 134
(6) See Pl. XXXI for an earlier example.

PLATE L

KUNG, A CYLINDRICAL CUP WITH RING HANDLE AND LID

Green
Ming-Ch'ing period (ca. 17th century A.D.)
H. 4 1/4 in.   *B60 J203*

This is a late version of a type of vessel that has been discussed at some length in connection with the cup shown in Plate XXXVI. Here also the main field is occupied by a phoenix confronting a feline. As it is done in low relief this main motif stands out far more clearly than in the earlier piece. The sparse spiralled grain pattern in the background is of Warring States origin[1] and rather unusual in this context. The narrow neck and foot bands, as well as the side of the lid, are decorated with C-shapes in thread relief. The three feet are in the form of animal masks with curious ears that look like nail heads. Similar masks are incised on the lid and on the top of the ring handle. Also, on top of the lid are three birds carved almost in the round and a spool-like knob. A cup comparable to this one was unearthed in 1962 in a tomb located in the western suburbs of Peking. The tomb in question is dated 1676.[2]

This cup bears no less than three inscriptions; a one-character inscription on the lid which is a conventionalized version of the character *Shou* for longevity, a three-character one on the base of the vessel meaning: "Cup of Long Happiness"[3] and a twenty-character dedicatory inscription inside the lid. This last inscription is carved in archaic script and imitates those that are sometimes found on ancient bronze vessels.

(1) Cf. Pls. XIII, XIV and XV.
(2) *Wen Wu*, 1963, no. 1, p. 42, fig. 18
(3) According to the *Shuo Wen*, the term *kung* designated originally a wine cup made of horn of a female rhinoceros. The same term can also be read *Kuang* and this second reading has been adopted by modern archeologists to designate one type of ancient bronze vessels. (Cf. for instance, d'Argencé, *A.B.C. Bronzes*, Pls. XX and XXI)

114

PLATE LI

PAIR OF LOTUS PODS WITH DRAGON-FLY AND PRAY-ING MANTIS

Greyish green with brown markings
Early to Mid Ch'ing Period (17th-18th century A.D.)
L. 7 in.   *B60 J443*

At first glance this subject may seem to belong to the same category with the Buddha's hand illustrated in Pl. XLVI.   In fact, the nature of the jade, the highly polished surface, the sharpness of the carving, a certain mannerism in the disposition of the leaves and the pseudo-anecdotic character of the scene, all speak in favor of a much later date.   The insects were included to add a touch of actuality and also of virtuosity.

All these traits are typical of the Ch'ing approach, so is the fact that the object was not meant to be used in any other way than as an object d'art in the modern sense of the term.

The lotus is the sacred flower of Buddhism, probably because it vaguely resembles the Wheel of the Law.   In this context it symbolizes "purity and perfection because it grows out of mud, but is not defiled, just as Buddha is born into the world but lives above the world; and because its fruits are said to be ripe when the flower blooms, just as the truth preached by Buddha bears immediately, the fruit of enlightenment."[1]

In Taoist symbolism, too, the lotus is frequently used as the attribute of one of the Eight Immortals.   The large number of seeds contained in the pods is also regarded as an emblem of copious posterity.

(1)   Williams quoting Anesaki in *Outlines*, p. 257.

PLATE LII

HU-SHAPED VASE WITH ELEPHANT-HEAD HANDLES

Green
Ch'ing period, Ch'ien Lung style (18th Century A.D.*)*
H. 8 1/8 in.

B60 J496

Emperor Ch'ien Lung's own taste and interest were largely responsible for the third and main wave of archaism which influenced jade carvers as well as other artists during most of the 18th and 19th centuries. Unlike the sporadic and hesitating endeavors of the Late Medieval[1] and Ming[2] periods this one was massive and sophisticated. Ancient bronze vessels served as favorite models either for imitations or more frequently for adaptations that could be highly imaginative.

The contours of this monumental vase were inspired by the rather classical shape of a type of ancient bronze vessel known as *hu*[3] but the handles are borrowed from contemporary (i.e. 18th century A.D.) ceramics.[4] The decoration, too, is a marvel of studied anachronism. Most of the motives that appear in the central zone[5] and its two marginal bands[6] can be traced back to the Bronze Age. The same applies to the hanging blades incised on the neck. Conversely, the leaf-shaped raised band around the foot is derived from the Yüan or Early Ming repertoire.[7]

Jade carvers of the Ch'ien Lung period were not only astute amalgamators, they were also unparalleled transposers. It has been said quite often that their transpositions and adaptations were the result of misconceptions. To the careful observer, however, they frequently appear as calligraphic masterpieces. Here, for instance, practically every single element of the central *t'ao-t'ieh* mask is rendered by means of curved lines and spirals to match the sweeping contours of the vessel and the rest of the decor. It looks as though a typically frontal and static motif of the Shang and Early Western Chou periods had been imparted with a Mid or Late Western Chou rhythm.[8]

The collection possesses another vase of the same type, which is dated 1789.[9] It has lug handles instead of elephant head ring handles. Its decoration also presents minor variations but it is, otherwise, very close to the one discussed here. One curious feature shared by the two vessels and also by many archaistic vessels of the period is the presence of claws in the region of the eyes of the monster's mask. This seems to be an 18th century innovation.

(1) Cf. Plate XXX
(2) Cf. Pl. XXXVIII
(3) Cf. d'Argencé, *A.B.C. Bronzes*, Pls. XXXIV, B and XLII, B
(4) Cf. Jenyns, *Later Chinese Porcelain*, Pl. XCIX 2 and P. J. Donnelly, *Blanc de Chine*, New York, 1967, Pl. 54, B.
(5) For a prototype of this *t'ao-t'ieh* mask see d'Argencé, *A.B.C. Bronzes*, Pl. XXIV, A
(6) For early examples of whorl circles see d'Argencé, *A.B.C. Bronzes*, Pls. III and XXVII, B.
(7) In effect this is a somewhat debased version of the leaf border incised on the lid of the *tou*-shaped cup illustrated in Pl. XXXVIII
(8) See for instance, d'Argencé, *A.B.C. Bronzes*, Pl. XXXIV, B and XXXVI, C for illustrations of the rhythm in question.
(9) See d'Argencé, *A.B.C. Chinese Treasures*, Pl. 51

PLATE LIII

INCENSE BURNER IN THE SHAPE OF A SQUARE TING

White, mutton-fat type
Ch'ing period, Ch'ien Lung style (18th century A.D.)
H. 6 in.   *B60 J20*

Inspired by a shape that was first conceived of by bronze-casters of the Early Western Chou period[1] the Ch'ing lapidary has created a vessel which is all at once novel and faithful to its model.

The traditional elements are best illustrated by the general structure of the container, the quasi-anatomical distribution of the ornamentation[2] and the choice of motives of decoration.   Conversely, the large S-shaped handles, the cylinders that link them to the mouth rim, the lid with its high and voluminous knob and the details in the ornamentation are all novelties.

T'ao-t'ieh masks of this period are usually so dissolved that the central shield becomes a separate geometric motif with little or no connection with the other elements of the masks.[3]   At the same time, the artist who designed this mask made his own the well-known ambiguity which prevailed in Shang times when the the *t'ao-t'ieh* would simultaneously look like a frontal mask and like two confronted dragons seen in profile[4].   Only here, the craftsman has "birdicized" the dragons.[5] The sturdy and rectilinear flanges of old also underwent drastic changes.   Split in half they assume spiraling contours which look like cursive variants of the *fu* (power to judge) sign in the time-honored group of symbols known as the "Twelve Ornaments".[6]

The legs, most of the handles and the rims of the containers and lid were left plain in order to let the superior stone speak for itself.   In those days white jade was more prized than any other kind.

(1)   Cf. d'Argencé, *A.B.C. Bronzes*, Pls. XXVIII and XXIX
(2)   Cf. *ibid.*, p. 14
(3)   See also Pls. LII, LIV and LVIII
(4)   Cf. *A.B.C. Bronzes*, Pl. IV, B
(5)   See, *ibid.*, Pl. XVII for a forerunner of the present motif.   The jade carver has attempted to reintegrate what was once completely dissolved.
(6)   See Yetts, *Symbolism*, pp. 12 and 13 and Margaret Medley, *A Handbook of Chinese Art*, London 1964, pp. 102, 103

PLATE LIV

KUEI-SHAPED INCENSE BURNER

Translucent light green
Ch'ing period, Ch'ien Lung style (18th century A.D.*)*
H. 6 1/2 in. B60 J25 +

Some of the most typical and spectacular innovations of the 18th century succeeded in rejuvenating ancient bronze shapes. These are by no means servile copies. On the contrary they stand out as the unequalled products of imaginations that were fired by the antiquarian spirit prevailing during the period in question.[1]

The basic shape of this vessel goes back to the Late Western Chou and its surface decoration is remotely derived from the Late Shang or Early Western Chou[2] repertoire.[3] The bird handles recall the phoenixes found on some medieval victory cups.[4] The feet and the dragon-shaped knob of the lid are outright 18th century novelties.

Such audacious juxtapositions would necessarily create a feeling of uneasiness if they had not been completely assimilated and translated into an entirely new and highly original idiom. This unprecedented faculty of blending and modernizing ancient styles constitutes one of the main contributions of the workshops patronized by Ch'ien Lung and his entourage. This is not an isolated phenomenon since some of the most prominent painters and potters of the Ch'ing dynasty spent their lives in the pursuit of antiquity.

The decorative motives incised on the body and lid of the vessel are centered on "birdicized" *t'ao-t'ieh* masks which resemble those of the preceding item. Here, however, we face a compounded ambiguity. The central shield, finally liberated, has become a mask in its own right, as can be seen from the presence of two diminutive eyes on either side of the central ridge.

Published: L. Sickman, *Selections from the Avery Brundage Collection*, San Francisco, 1960, fig. 35

(1) See Pl. LII and LIII.
(2) Cf. d'Argencé, *A.B.C. Bronzes*, Pl. XXXIV, D.
(3) Cf. *ibid.*, Pl. IV, B.
(4) Cf. Pl. XXX.

PLATE LV

TWO INCENSE BURNERS IN THE SHAPE OF COLOR-MIXERS

Dark green and white
Late Ch'ing period (18th–19th century A.D.*)*
Both are 5 1/4 in. high   *B60 J17 (white) B60 J18 (green)*

These vessels look like rectangles with cylindrical and projecting corners. Such unusual shapes are derived from bronze color mixers of the Warring States or Han period[1] and seem to have been in great demand during the later part of the Ch'ing dynasty.

Besides their general silhouettes the vessels have several important features in common: the division of the ornamentation into horizontal bands, the squatting dragons that serve as lid knobs, the coiling *ch'ih*[2] which adorn the top of the cylinders and the auspicious characters that are carved in relief on the central panels. One of these characters, on the green vessel, is carved in pseudo-archaic bird-script and stands for "longevity". The other character (on the white vessel) stands for "happiness". Obviously such vessels were made as gifts to commemorate some happy occasion.

The squatting dragons present the peculiarity of being supported by free-sculptured spirals that resemble a coiled spring or an old-fashioned corkscrew.

The monumental two-spiralled handles of the green vessel were probably inspired by prototypes dating back to the Mid or Late Medieval period.[3] With the exception of three narrow bands of compounded C-shaped spirals and bosses the rest of the ornmentation of this vessel consists either of dissolved animal shapes or of two auspicious Buddhist symbols, the swastika (with crampons directed towards the right) and the sauvastika (with crampons directed to the left).

The decoration of the white vessel is less homogeneous. The upper zone is filled with an interlacery of snakes curiously shown in profile, but with their heads upside down. Less acrobatic prototypes of this theme date back to the Ch'un-ch'iu or Early Warring States period.[4] The dragon-head ring handles can claim an even more ancient ancestry.[5] The cylindrical parts of the lower zone are more prosaically decorated with stylized floral motifs.

(1) See *Wen Wu Ts'an K'ao Tzu Liao*, 1958, no. 11, p. 77, fig. 1.
(2) Cf. Pls. XIV, XXXVII, XXXIX.
(3) See Pl. XXXVI.
(4) See for instance, d'Argencé, *A.B.C. Bronzes*, Pl. XXXVIII.
(5) See *ibid.*, Pl. XXXI for an Early Western Chou prototype.

124

PLATE LVI

SQUARE TSUN-SHAPED VASE WITH ARCHAISTIC DECOR

Mottled dark green with black specks and purple markings
Late Ch'ing period (18th-19th century A.D.)
H. 10 1/4 in.   *B60 J21+*

So far all our archaistic examples of the Ch'ing period remained fairly faithful to their models.[1]   This vessel, however, is more an adaptation than an imitation. The general contours are inspired by those of a type of bronze vessel that was made during the 10th century B.C.[2] but with so many modifications that the analogy is no longer evident.   The straight neck with the square and slightly flaring mouth is just as unexpected as the curvature of the foot.   The most obviously conservative feature rests with the presence of structural flanges[3] even if these are zoomorphic.

Each side of the neck is decorated with a large animal head holding a ring in the mouth.   The rest of the ornamentation consists of several variants of a long-tailed, long-crested bird which first appeared on bronze vessels of the Late Shang or Early Western Chou periods.[4]

These flamboyant motifs and the unusually deep carving give a slightly baroque touch to this otherwise solidly classical vessel.

(1)   See Pls. LII to LV
(2)   Cf. d'Argencé, *A.B.C. Bronzes*, Pl. XXX
(3)   *ibid.*, p. 10
(4)   See for instance *Osaka-San Francisco Exchange Exhibition*, p. 118, no. 67.

PLATE LVII

RHYTON RESTING ON INVERTED MONSTER HEAD

White with iron rust markings
Mid Ch'ing period (ca. 18th century A.D.*)*
H. 8 1/4 in.   *B61 J1+*

Here is an 18th century version of an already familiar category.[1]   The vessel stands squarely on a slightly concave base and its contours are of a smooth regularity which reveals that the carvers are now quite at ease with this challenging shape.

The inverted monster's mask, which occupies the lower part of the cup, is in many respects similar to those of the *hu*-shaped vessel shown in Plate LII.   At the same time it presents at least three unusual features, two pairs of formidable fangs, disconnected claws that are located on the back of the head and two very large *ling-chih*-shaped excrescences which could be interpreted as overgrown ears.

The ornamentation of the neck band consists of two confronted dragons in raised lines.

When compared with that of Plate XXXVII the *ch'ih* which climbs along one side of the vessel looks considerably more mature.   Its head, neck and shoulders are all above the rim of the vase—so are the three-clawed forepaws.   In addition to the usual flame-like incisions on the shoulders and hips, the sides are flanked by almost free-sculpted spiraling appendages which are probably conventionalized wings.

On the other side a deeply carved animal head holds a ring in its mouth.   With its bifurcated horns, its finely striated mane, its tripartite forehead, its comma-shaped eyeballs and its depressed nose bridge with flat, large nostrils, this head stands out as the most archaistic feature of the whole vessel.

(1)   See Pls. XXXIV, XXXVII, XLIX

Plate LVIII

KUANG-SHAPED VESSEL

Mottled greyish white with brown and black markings
Mid Ch'ing dynasty (18th century A.D.*)*
H. 9 in.   *B60 J28*

The *kuang* was a rare shape among ancient bronze vessels[1] and an even rarer one among jade archaistic vessels. Despite its flattened and elogated proportions the silhouette of this vase remains fairly close to those of bronze prototypes. As usual, however, the 18th century carver has recreated an ornamentation which owes little if anything to Late Shang or Early Western Chou specimens. Especially noticeable is the absence of that curious association of quadrupeds and birds which is the hallmark of Bronze Age *kuang*.

On the body of the vase the decoration is done in raised line and low relief. It consists of large flamboyant *t'ao-t'ieh* masks with elements resembling bats' wings for the central zone, and of subtly animalized hanging and rising blades for the foot and neck zones respectively. The massive handle is made of a monster's head devouring a reptile with a small dorsal fin. The front part of the lid is incised with a bovine mask while its ridge is topped by a strange creature with the tail of a fish, a body resembling a fin and two conventionalized flowers for a head.

Published: d'Argencé, *Apollo*, p. 139, fig. 5 (a)
(1) See *A.B.C. Bronzes*, pp. 50–53.

130

Plate LIX

CH'IU-SHAPED RHYTON

Green with extensive brown markings
Ch'ing dynasty, Ch'ien Lung period, dated mid-spring 1785 A.D.
H. 5 1/2 in.   *B60 J466*

This rhyton presents several very unusual features, including a dated 37-character imperial inscription delicately incised on the flat base. The bulk of this inscription consists of a poem which can be translated as follows:

"It has spent a thousand autumns in the Khotan river. The vapors of the water and the chemicals of the soil have soaked into it without excess. (It makes us) reject the vulgar and the biased and teaches us to imitate the ancient. In singing the praises of this *ch'iu* we cannot differentiate it from a Han vessel."

The poem is followed by the date, the imperial signature and one of Ch'ien Lung's seals.

Ch'iu, the word used by the Emperor to designate the vessel, is a rare one which suggests a container made of horn. In fact, it is one of several vocables corresponding more or less to our term "rhyton." [1]

Ch'ien Lung's supposition that this object was carved from a pebble seems to be well founded. The artist obviously did his utmost to respect the original contours of the stone.

The upper part of the vessel is decorated with three bands of geometric designs, all incised and all borrowed from the Bronze Age repertoire. A large band of interlocked T-shaped spirals is framed at the top by a narrow belt, square meanders and at the bottom by another narrow belt simulating a twisted rope.

As in most other rhytons the foot of the vessel assumes the shape of a monster's head. [2] This particular head is partly reversible, but reads best when the vessel is turned upside down. [3] The mouth is wide open and stretches over the entire width of the base.

Both the head and the available space in the median field of the vessel are adorned with a "spiral-and-eye" pattern, which is undoubtedly inspired by a standard Warring States design. [4] Here, however, the slightly zoomorphic shapes of old have been replaced by volutes suggesting *ju-i* heads [5] and consequently symbolizing longevity.

Published: Hartman, *Chinese Jade of Five Centuries*, Pl. 44

(1) Cf. Pl. XXXIV.
(2) Cf. Pls. XXXVII, LVII, LXXVII.
(3) The reversible head is by no means a new idea. See for instance the belt-hook illustrated in the upper right corner of Pl. XVII.
(4) Cf. Pl. XIV.
(5) So called because they resemble the heads of *ju-i* sceptres, which in turn imitate the shape of *ling-chih* fungus. Cf. Pls. XLII, XLIII and LXXIX.

PLATE LX

KUEI-SHAPED INCENSE BURNER

Ch'ing Period, Ch'ien Lung style (18th century A.D.*)*
H. 5 3/4 in. W. 8 1/3 in. B62 J66

During the 18th century court taste became extremely eclectic under the influence of Emperor Ch'ien Lung himself. Color began to be as important as shape and ornamentation and lapidaries frequently resorted to a variety of stones producing color effects never seen in jade. Lapis lazuli, a deep blue crystalline limestone usually speckled with light brown or yellow, is one of them. Most of the lapis lazuli carved in China was imported from Tibet and from Afghanistan via Chinese Turkestan.

This *kuei* is much closer to bronze prototypes than a comparable vessel illustrated Pl. LIV[1], even though the oversized knob of the lid and handles are typical 18th century features. The ornamentation on the body is done in low relief and incisions. It is very minute and delicate and consists of four circular bands: one on the top of the knob, another one on the side of the lid, a third one on the concave shoulder and a fourth one on the belly proper. The last band is also the largest one. It shows on each side a large and fairly coherent *t'ao-t'ieh* mask flanked by highly dissolved *k'uei* dragons with gaping mouths. The ornamentation of the shoulder band is made of a central whorl circle flanked by confronted crouching dragons with spiralling crests and elongated bifid tails[2] The central *t'ao-t'ieh* masks of the lid are highly simplified and almost lose their identity in a maze of vegetable *ju-i*, animal eyes, claws and geometric shapes, which have some affinities with part of the decoration of the preceding *ch'iu*-shaped vessel and proceed from the same source[3]. The annular band of the knob consists of similarly dissolved geometric and animal patterns, including the usual disconnected claws.

The massive, partly openwork handles are typical 18th century concoctions. Two enormous dragon heads are supported by atrophic bodies with abdominal fins and tripartite tails, one of the branches being in the shape of a small crested bird's head.

(1)   Cf. for instance, Jung Keng, *Shang Chou Ch'i T'ung K'ao*, Peking, 1941, Pl. 278.
(2)   See the *chih*-shaped cup, Pl. XXXVIII, for an earlier example of the same motif
(3)   See note (5), preceding caption

PLATE LXI

BRUSH HOLDER (PI T'UNG)

Spinach green with black specks
Mid Ch'ing period (18th century A.D.)
H. 7 in. Diam. 8 in. B60 J29

Just as their Warring States predecessors had invented a larger number of objects specifically designed to embellish the warrior's equipment,[1] the Ch'ing carvers produced many new objects to adorn the writer's desk. Some of these objects —brush holders, table screens, mountains—attain unusually large dimensions. Many illustrate religious or profane scenes in full-fledged landscape settings, thus marking the culmination of a trend whose origin can be traced back to the Ming dynasty.[2]

In a broader context, this is the last stage in the thematic development of Chinese jades which has been described elsewhere as a gradual conquest of the universe[3] starting with zoomorphs and successively incorporating human representations,[4] plants[5] and finally the whole of nature (inhabited landscapes).

Many landscapes carved on jade were inspired by paintings on silk, paper or other materials, notably ceramics.

The entire surface of this thick-walled, five-footed cylinder is decorated with a continuous scene showing a procession of ten horsemen riding along a mountain path that leads to a temple half-hidden in the distance. Six of the horsemen ride two by two at more or less lengthy intervals. Some carry quivers full of arrows and one holds a falcon. They seem to act as the escort of the central group that consists of four riders, two carrying banners, one a *ju-i* scepter and one a vase containing three ceremonial halberds. The last two riders and their attributes form one of the numerous rebused messages concocted by Ming and Ch'ing designers.[6] In spoken Chinese "to be on horseback" (*ma shang*) also means "promptly", "vase" (*p'ing*) is homonymous with "peace", "three halberds" (*san chi*) with "three classes" and the *ju-i* sceptre is equivalent to "as you wish".[7] Taken as a whole these various symbols and associations of ideas would mean: "(may) you rapidly and according to (your) desire (attain) peace and (complete) the three classes (of official-dom)". The background is occupied by a vast stretch of water, perhaps a lake or a large river and a chain of mountains. The foreground is made of rocky cliffs and of luxuriant trees. This short, circular "handscroll" is topped by a narrow band of clouds that run along the mouthrim.

Published: Gump, *Jade, Stone of Heaven*, p. 168; d'Argencé, *Apollo*, p. 137, Pl. XV and *A.B.C. Chinese Treasures*, p. 62, Pl. 50

(1) See Pls. XIV and XVI.
(2) See Pl. XII.
(3) *A.B.C. Chinese Treasures*, p. 8.
(4) Cf. Pl. XIX and XX.
(5) Cf. Pl. XLVI.
(6) See for instance Pls. XLII, XLIII, XLVIII and LXXVIII.
(7) Cf. Pl. LXXIX.

PLATE LXII

BOWL WITH RING HANDLES

Mottled dark spinach green
Mid Ch'ing period (18th century A.D.)
Diam. 11 1/4 in.   *B60 J405*

As another example of 18th century eclecticism here is a bowl which shows a certain amount of Western influence, not so much in the shape, which remains fairly traditional, as in the ornamentation which is exclusively and boldly floral.

The same flower, the chrysanthemum, symbol of autumn and joviality, is used in scroll form on the side and in medallion form in the bottom. In both cases the flowers are rendered in unusually precise and high undercut relief. The ring handles, too, are topped by chrysanthemum buds in the round.

The entire bowl, including the ring handles, was carved from one piece of jade.

Spinach jade, (*po-ts'ai yü* in Chinese), owes its name to the presence of numerous jet-black specks imbedded in the dark green stone. Seemingly of Siberian origin, it was particularly sought after by carvers of the 18th and 19th centuries.

PLATE LXIII

BRUSH HOLDERS IN SHAPE OF A TREE-TRUNK AND OF CLIFFS WITH PLANTS

The light grey one with white markings is jade
The black one is delessite, an iron-rich chlorite
Mid to Late Ch'ing period (18th-19th century A.D.*)*
Respectively 4 5/8 in. and 4 1/8 in. high   B60 J229 and B60 J202

Brush holders in the shape of cylindrical tree-trunks or rocky cliffs with plants and branches of withered old trees were much in favor among scholars of the 18th and 19th centuries.[1]

The light grey piece is another example of the unsurpassed degree of sophistication attained by 18th and 19th century carvers. When looking at an object of this kind where the decoration is almost all done in the round, one is apt to overlook the fact that jade is one of the hardest minerals on earth. Without succeeding altogether to avoid a certain amount of mannerism the artist has imparted to his subject a good deal of dynamic humor. Beyond the obvious game of hide and seek there is the usual interplay of symbolic values, the pine being regarded as an emblem of longevity and the monkey as an animal capable of bestowing "health, protection and success on mankind".[2]

The most remarkable feature about the other brush holder is the almost jet-black quality of its texture. Delessite is one of the minerals jade carvers resorted to when they had to produce certain color effects which never occurred in jade.[3] Besides a very indented profile which is meant to suggest complex rock formations, the ornamentation consists primarily of *ling-chih* fungi and of the gnarled blossoming branches of an old plum tree and of bamboos. *Ling-chih*, plum blossoms and bamboos are regarded in various degrees as symbols of longevity. Furthermore, the plum is an emblem of winter.

(1) See for instance, "The Arts of the Ch'ing Dynasty", *T.O.C.S.*, 1963/64, vol. 35, figs. 311, 417 and 422.
(2) Williams, *Outlines*, p. 278
(3) See Pl. LX

140

PLATE LXIV

MOUNTAIN

Lapis Lazuli
Ch'ing period, Ch'ien Lung style (18th century A.D.*)*
H. 9 1/4 in. W. 13 in.   *B60 J31*

According to Chinese literature, miniature mountains were carved out of jade as early as the Yüan dynasty[1] but, so far, no extant specimen can be dated with any certainty prior to the Ch'ing dynasty.

The majority of these mountains serve as grandiose settings for scenes of Taoist or Buddhist inspiration.   The largest one, located in the Forbidden City of Peking, is known as the "Great Yü Mountain".   It is 7 feet high, 3 feet across and is said to weigh at least seven tons.[2]

One side of the present object shows a bearded immortal and his young servant gathering fungi of immortality (*ling-chih*)[3] that grow on a narrow and rather vertiginous ledge over a subterranean river.   Roofs of large buildings appear in the distance immediately above the main scene, while the rest of the landscape contains several symbols of longevity, including a crane and pine trees.   Similar trees appear on the reverse in association with deer which are supposed to be the only animals capable of finding the fungus of immortality.   One of the flat rocks on the obverse bears a forty-nine character inscription.   Incised and filled with gold paint, it reproduces a poem written by Ch'ien Lung himself.   In this poem the Emperor comments on a landscape entitled "Immortal gathering the fungus of immortality in the mountain" and painted by the famous 16th century artist Ch'iu Ying.

Published: d'Argencé, *A.B.C. Chinese Treasures,* Pl. 52; Rawson and Ayers, *Chinese Jade,* no. 494
(1)   Cf. Hansford, *Chinese Jade Carving,* p. 76.
(2)   See John Goette, *Jade Lore,* New York, 1936, pp. 180 ff.
(3)   Cf. Pl. XLIII.

142

Plate LXV

MOUNTAIN

Spinach green
Mid Ch'ing period (18th century A.D.)
H: 8 in. W: 10 in.   *B60 J49*

Both sides of this mountain show various moments of a great hunt which takes place amidst the most luxuriant vegetation. The obverse is divided into three horizontal fields. At the top two horsemen are engaged in hot pursuit after a deer. The middle field shows what seems to be the same hunters and the same deer, only closer to one another and preceded by a panther. The bottom field is also the widest. It contains two groups of hunters, including two falconers, one archer and one halberdier.

The composition of the reverse is axed on a diagonal and based on a single theme, that of the successful hunting party returning home. See frontispiece.

Technically, as well as iconographically, this piece is very close to the brush holder of Plate LXI. One is tempted to think that both objects were produced by the same workshop.

144

PLATE LXVI

MINIATURE MOUNTAINS

On the left, Saussuritized Gabbro, light grey with black and purple markings.
Early to Mid Ch'ing period (17th-18th century A.D.*)*
H. 5 in.   B60 J474
On the right, Lapis Lazuli
Mid Ch'ing period, Ch'ien Lung style (18th century A.D.*)*
H. 6 3/8 in.   B60 J461

The recto of the lapis lazuli is carved with a variant of the theme described in connection with Plate LXIV while that of the other piece shows more prosaically an old scholar and his young servant approaching a waterfall. The servant carries a *ch'in* (lute) which in those days was regarded by scholars as an indispensable piece of equipment because its harmonies blended well with the voices of nature and, particularly, of flowing water and whispering pine trees.

The versos of both pieces are replete with symbols of longevity: two cranes and pine trees for the lapis lazuli; two cranes, a large *ling-chih* fungus and a *Wu-t'ung* tree for the saussuritized gabbro. The *wu-t'ung* or *Dryandra cordifolia*, is supposedly the only tree on which the phoenix would alight. Its large leaves are highly ornamental.

146

PLATE LXVII

MOUNTAIN. P'U-HSIEN PAYING A VISIT TO WEN-SHU

Light green with brown markings
Early to Mid Ch'ing period (17th-18th century A.D.)
H. 6 3/4 in. W. 9 in.   B60 J26

This last example out of the large group of miniature mountains that are part of the Collection[1] illustrates a well-known Buddhist theme. P'u-hsien, or Samantabhadra in Sanskrit, the Bodhisattva of Benevolence pays a visit to Wen-shu (Manjusri), the Bodhisattva of Wisdom. In more hieratic representations these deities stand on either side of Buddha to form one of the classical triads.

In this slightly facetious representation, P'u-hsien, mounted on his elephant, holding a *ju-i* sceptre[2] and accompanied by an attendant who carries the sacred umbrella, has just reached the bottom of a stairway which probably leads to his heavenly retreat. A well-fed Wen-shu sits in meditation in his cave, which is surrounded by a palatial balustrade. His young attendant is walking his usual mount, a lion.

The verso shows a mountain scene with deep grottoes, pine trees and a tall, hexagonal, three-storied pagoda.

Published: d'Argencé, *Asia Foundation*, fig. 17; *Apollo*, p. 139, fig. 5; *A.B.C. Chinese Treasures*, Pl. 42

(1)   See also Pls. LXIV, LXV and LXVI.
(2)   Cf. Pls. XLII, LXI and LXXIX.

PLATE LXVIII

CIRCULAR TABLE SCREEN

Dark spinach green
Mid to Late Ch'ing period (18th-19th century A.D.)
Diam. 10 1/2 in.   B60 J22 +

Round or square screens for the writer's desk can be considered as one of the main contributions of Ch'ing lapidary art.[1]   Carved on both sides, they were mounted in wooden or metallic stands that could be as elaborately decorated as the screens themselves.

This piece is carved in high undercut relief.   The unusually fine workmanship is characterized by bold, dynamic compositions and a great precision in the execution of all the details.

One side is decorated with a pair of crested pheasants perched on a gnarled and blossoming plum tree.[2]   The other side is all but filled with large tree peonies which are a sign of spring, as well as an emblem of affection and good fortune.

The analogy with contemporaneous painting is striking, not just because of the themes involved or the format, which recalls a type of round album leaves, but principally because the carver has succeeded in capturing the flowing, sensitive and incisive brush strokes of his painted model.

(1)   Cf. Pl. LXI
(2)   Cf. Pl. LXIII

PLATE LXIX

FLOWER OR JOSS-STICK HOLDER IN THE FORM OF A RECLINING BULL

Translucent light green with brown markings
Ch'ing period, Ch'ien Lung style (18th century A.D.)
L. 5 1/2 in.   *B60 J237*

The wave of archaism, which marked the 18th century and particularly Ch'ien Lung's reign,[1] extended to many animal types as well.

This bull holds its head slightly raised and turned almost all the way back. Double incisions with spiraling endings mark the tightly closed mouth. The nostrils are rendered by small raised circles with central depressions. The protuberant, conical eyes have three creased eyelids and seem to be suffering from severe cross-eyed strabismus. The ears are tubular and the horns flat, slightly curved and pointed. The hooves are cloven and carved with great care, including the undersides. The two-stepped tail is more ovine than bovine. The spine is left plain, but the animal carries two contiguous containers on its back—one is cylindrical and the other one rectangular. Shoulders and haunches are emphasized by bold spirals in high relief.

The posture of this half mythical creature, the shape and position of its horns and ears and the intricate network of incised spirals that cover it from head to tail are traits which could easily be traced back to the earliest periods of Chinese art.[2]

At the same time the nature of the stone and the quality of the workmanship are unmistakably Ch'ing. Indeed, practically all the characteristics listed above could also serve to describe a well-known champlevé bull dated Ch'ien Lung and belonging to the Victoria and Albert Museum in London.[3] The resemblance is too striking to be accidental. This is undoubtedly one of the numerous cases when the 18th century jade carver looked for inspiration in objects made according to the cloisonné or champlevé techniques.

(1) Cf. Pl. LII
(2) See for instance L. Sickman and A. Soper, *The Art and Architecture of China*, Penguin, 1960, Pl. 2 (B), illustrating a white marble water-buffalo of the Shang dynasty.
(3) See Jenyns and Watson, *Chinese Art, The Minor Arts*, New York, 1963, Pl. 84.

PLATE LXX

DRAGONIZED CARPS RISING FROM THE WATER

Deep green with brown markings
Mid Ch'ing period (18th century A.D.)
H. 7 1/4 in.   *B60 J446*

Facing each other, one large and one small dragon-headed carps leap from the water. The oversized, scaleless heads have openwork mouths with cylindrical apertures, two pairs of fangs and semi-circular saw-tooth borders. The heart-shaped noses are characterized by spiraling nostrils and sunken bridges. Sinuous and elongated whiskers cross over the open mouths, run along the lower jaws and end up in spirals. The small, pin-like eyeballs are set in elongated V-shaped sockets. The shallow bumpy foreheads are buried under saw-toothed fringes. Two soft, two-pointed antlers for the large carp and one spiraling horn for the small one rest on the nape above ears of the "spiral-and-point" type.[1] Manes consist of a single striated tuft, gills are marked by grooves and wavy goatees adhere to the chins.

With the exception of the bellies that are ribbed, the bodies are covered with rounded scales that are incised with elongated V-shaped lines. The fins and tails are in the shape of stylized and oversized *ling-chih* fungi,[2] but dorsals are shallow and marked with sharp undulations. The base is made of tiny rocks and of a concave whirlpool extending in small finger-like waves.

Legend has it that the Yellow River carps which make their way up stream and succeed in passing above the rapids of Lung-men (Dragon Gate) in Honan become transformed into dragons. These carps are also compared to students who pass their examinations with distinction and are consequently regarded as a symbol of literary success.

(1) Compare with Pl. XVIII.
(2) Cf. Pl. XLIII.

Plate LXXI

PAIR OF MANDARIN DUCKS

Light green and lustrous
Ch'ing dynasty, probably Ch'ien Lung period (18th century A.D.)
L. 6 1/4 in.   *B60 J442*

The birds form an inseparable pair.   The larger one looks all the way back towards its companion and both hold the same stalk of blossoming lotus in their beaks.

Heads and bodies are rendered in a cubic manner that suggests some metallic models.   The sides are flattened and all contours are treated geometrically, especially those of the jaws and beaks that look as if they had been squared off with a hatchet.   The wings consist of three consecutive zones.   The shoulders are decorated with the silhouettes of conventionalized ducks framed by arabesques while the second and third zones are made of square meanders.   The tails are outlined by a band made of similar square meanders.

By contrast the claw-like waves and the slightly more formalized lotus stalk are all at once much more naturalistic and cursive.

The time-honored theme of the quadruped, fish or bird holding a plant in its mouth or beak[1] is revived here in a curiously roundabout way since the carver was obviously inspired by a contemporaneous model in bronze or cloisonné.

The necklace of the larger bird is a very tale-telling detail.   Necklaces worn by birds are traced back to at least the Han dynasty[2] but this particular ornament with its row of stylized flowers is typical of the 18th century's repertory of motives.[3]

Mandarin ducks are famous for the beauty of their plumage.   When shown in pairs they symbolize conjugal bliss because of the remarkable attachment they show to each other.   This theme is, perhaps, best known through Early Ming examples in blue-and-white porcelain.[4]   Through one of those associations of ideas that are typical of the Chinese mind, the lotus has become a symbol of abundant progeny.[5]   This kind of carving would, therefore, be a very appropriate gift to make to a newly married couple.

(1) Cf. Pls. XLIII and XLV.
(2) Cf. Pl. XXIV.
(3) See *National Palace Museum Illustrated Handbook*, Taipei, 1967, fig. 134 for an example in cloisonné with a Ch'ien Lung mark.
(4) See *A.B.C. Chinese Ceramics*, Pl. L (D).
(5) See Nozaki M. *Kisshō Zuan Kaidai, Shina Fūzoku no Ichi Kenkyū*, Tientsin, 1928, pp. 376–380.

Plate LXXII

DRAGON RISING OVER THE WAVES

Light green and lustrous
Mid Ch'ing period (18th century A.D.*)*
H. 6 in.   *B60 J63*

Such technical tours de force best exemplify the incredible degree of virtuosity attained by some 18th century workshops. These prodigious craftsmen treated jade as though it were the most malleable material.

Dragons were frequently chosen as central motives for the ornamentation of objects destined to court officials. These sturdy animals differ from the lithe, wiry and dishevelled creatures of former times.[1] They are more stately, more earthly, also more imposing, almost menacing. With their square shoulders, their paws firmly planted on the ground (or on the clouds) and their enormous mouths showing bare teeth, they seem to be in perpetual posture of combat. Eighteenth century dragons are usually equipped with two-pointed antlers, bifurcated manes, voluminous beards and interminable whiskers with spiraling extremities.[2]

This dragon of the sea (*li*) chases a flaming whirlpool which has been variously interpreted as the sun, the moon or the "pearl of potentiality". It appears to be a symbol of the changing nature of dragons and ultimately of the ever-changing nature of life itself.

The openwork is so bold that the object is really a small sculpture in the round. A circular hole was bored in the base to facilitate the carving.

(1)   See for instance Pls. XV, XXXVII, XL
(2)   See also Pl. LV for variants of the same type.

PLATE LXXIII

SHAKYAMUNI AS AN ASCETIC

Light green and lustrous
Late Ch'ing period (18th–19th century A.D.)
H. 10 in.   *B60 J13*

Jade workshops of the Ch'ing dynasty were the first to produce human figurines in
large quantities.   The majority of these statuettes are of Buddhist and Taoist inspiration and quite a few of them attain impressive dimensions.

   The bulk of this production is mannered and, at times, frankly baroque, ex-
pecially during the last decades of the dynasty.   There are, however, exceptions
which reflect traditions that remain faithful to the spirit of the classical periods of
Chinese sculpture.

   The present effigy illustrates a phase of Shakyamuni's long search for enlightenment when the future Buddha spent several years in the jungle living the life of a
hermit.   The unusual, meditative posture, where the chin rests on the two hands,
which themselves rest on the raised left knee was apparently well established as a
standard iconographical feature for this particular subject as early as the Yüan dynasty.[1]   So were other minor details such as the elongated ears, the bald spot on the
head and the continuous frame of curls formed around the emaciated face by the
hair and beard.   In fact, this statuette corresponds almost line for line to a figure in
lacquered wood which belongs to the Detroit Institute of Arts and has been ascribed to the Yüan period.[2]

Published: Gump, *Jade, Stone of Heaven*, p. 53
(1)   Lee and Ho, *Chinese Art Under the Mongols: The Yüan Dynasty (1279–1368)*, Pls. 18–20
(2)   Idem., Pl. 20

PLATE LXXIV

KU-SHAPED VASE

Transparent light green
H. 11 in.   B60 J259

PLATE

Transparent milky white
Diam. 7 1/2 in. B60 J309

BOWL

Transparent green with black specks
Mid to Late Ch'ing period (18th–19th century A.D.)
Diam. 6 5/16 in.   B60 J149

The five objects shown here and on the following two plates illustrate another facet of the extraordinarily eclectic taste which prevailed during the Ch'ien Lung period and a good part of the 19th century.[1]   Despite their exceptionally fine quality such objects are rarely exhibited or published in the West.   They differ from all those we have discussed so far in more than one respect.   Their most outstanding characteristics are the extreme thinness of their walls, which makes them transparent; the elegant simplicity of their shape (at least for the present group) and the composition and nature of their ornamentation.   Decorative motives are essentially floral and are organized according to a strict, almost rigid, geometrical scheme.   They reflect in various degrees a taste which probably originated in 17th century India and became popular in China by the middle of the 18th century, as a result of interchanges of technical approaches and possibly also of craftsmen between the Chinese and the Mogul courts.   Usually a careful analysis of these objects leaves no doubt about their Chinese origin but an occasional border-line case can keep us wondering whether it was carved by Chinese or Indian hands.[2]

Outside of the general silhouette, little remains of the Late Shang bronze prototype which inspired the *ku*-shaped vase.[3]   Its trumpet is ribbed, its foot fluted and the whole of its ornamentation derived from that of blue-and-white and enameled porcelains of the Yung Cheng and Ch'ien Lung periods.[4]

In a manner which immediately brings to mind a typically Mogul mannerism, the floral designs that occupy so much space in the decoration of the white plate pay far greater attention to spiraling vines and tendrils than to the flowers proper.   The latter are conventionalized to the point of losing all vitality.   The outside of the bowl is decorated in low relief with a row of identical leafy flowers which are also derived from typical Mogul motives.[5]

(1)   Cf. Pl. LXII
(2)   See Pl. LXXVI
(3)   Cf. *A.B.C. Bronzes*, Pl. X
(4)   Cf. Jenyns, *Later Chinese Porcelain*, Pl. LXIII and *A.B.C. Ceramics*, Pl. LXXIV (A)
(5)   See for instance Stuart C. Welch, *The Art of Mughal India*, Asia House, 1963, Pls. 62 and 75

PLATE LXXV

DISH IN THE SHAPE OF STYLIZED LEAVES

Transparent light green
Mid-Late Ch'ing period (18th-19th century A.D.*)*
L. 10 in.   *B60 J7 +*

With this particularly frail and gracile example of what is known as Indian taste in Chinese jade[1] the receptacle itself consists of a cluster of five leaves. On the inside, delicate tendrils mark the ridges where the leaves overlap slightly. The handles, carved almost entirely in the round, are in the shape of withering flowers and, to complete the illusion, the feet are made of small leaves, which are tensely curved inwards.

Leaf-shaped and lobed drinking cups made of jade and other semi-precious stones, were much in favor at the Mogul court, the earliest dated specimens going back to the middle of the 17th century[2].

The present dish is completely sinicized, but a quick comparison with the deep bowl of Plate LXII will show that it remains outside the main tradition and still retains a certain foreign flavor.

(1) Cf. Pl. LXXIV
(2) Cf. Welch, *op. cit.* fig. 5; Monroe Wheeler, *Textiles and Ornaments of India*, New York, 1950, p. 76

PLATE LXXVI

COVERED BOXES

Transparent light green
Mogul or Chinese (18th-19th century A.D.)
L. 8 1/2 in. B60 J963

Seen from above the larger box looks like a rhomboid leaf with two pointed extremities. It does not communicate with the smaller box, the lid of which is linked to the body by means of a hinge. The boxes may have served to keep different kinds of sweetmeats. Both lids have knobs in the shape of budding flowers and are decorated with various blossoming sprays and leaf scrolls, while the base of the larger box is carved with a conventional floral motif. The collar and foot zones of the large box duplicate the outer band of the lid with a motif well attested in the decorative repertory of Mogul art.[1] The central zone of the same box is divided into twelve ogival arches where flowers alternate with genre scenes depicting, for the most part, couples drinking, playing games or making love.

The decoration of the smaller box is entirely floral, including the S-shaped handle which terminates at the lower end with a bud in what seems to be a typically Mogul mannerism.[2]

In fact, there is not a single element in the ornamentation of these boxes which does not bring to mind Mogul prototypes. Yet the crowded composition, the treatment of certain details, particularly the figures, and the shape themselves are not paralleled by any well-authenticated piece of Mogul jade, crystal or agate carving. Consequently one cannot ignore the possibility that these boxes might have been made in China for the foreign or even the domestic market.

(1) See Hansford, *Jade, Essence of Hills and Streams,* G14
(2) Welch, *The Art of Mughal India,* Pl. 51

166

PLATE LXXVII

RHYTON WITH ELEPHANT HEAD

White Chalcedony
H. 5 1/2 in.   *B60 J84*

WOMAN PLAYING WITH CHILD AND DOG

Turquoise
H. 2 1/2 in.   *B60 J830*

BELT HOOK WITH DRAGONS

Coral
L. 3 3/4 in.   *B60 J578*
All three objects can be ascribed to the Mid Ch'ing period (18th century A.D.*)*

Just like lapis lazuli and, for similar reasons,[1] a large number of semi-precious stones found their way to 18th century workshops. In their search for unusual colors, particularly for pure white, bright blue or bright red, lapidaries showed a marked preference for chalcedony, turquoise and coral.

The rhyton seems very close to the Late Medieval example of Plate XXXVIII. Minute inspection will reveal however that these objects differ widely in many respects. Far from being abstracted and slightly ambiguous, this elephant's head, with its leaf-like ears, its furrowed eyes and wrinkled chin recalls that of the very naturalistic, if decrepit, Ming or Early Ch'ing elephant of Plate XLIII. The dragons seem to form a family of two adults and two cubs. Despite their multi-branched tails and long-spiralling crests (or manes) they have lost almost entirely the feline quality of their forerunners and rather look like playful lizards.

Turquoise was very popular during the earliest periods of Chinese history when it may have been found locally.[2] After the Han, however, the only sources of supply seem to have been Mongolia and Tibet and the only dynasties who paid serious attention to the stone were the Yüan of Mongol stock and the Ch'ing of Manchu origin. This delightful group reflects a feminine taste rarely found in jade carvings and may have been just part of a set of statuettes picturing young ladies engaged in typical occupations.[3]

Many belt hooks of this type were carved in coral, jade or other hardstones during the 18th and 19th centuries. Usually they have become purely decorative objects. The carvers who made them did not hesitate, in true Ch'ing spirit, to domesticate, or even, at times emasculate the mythical animals which form the essential of their decoration. Here, facing the baroque dragon's head, a maneless and newt-like *ch'ih* carries in its mouth and on its back *ling-chih* fungi which are not usually found in this context.

(1) Cf. Pl. LX
(2) See *A.B.C. Bronzes*, pp. 54, 56, 114 and 130
(3) Cf. Jenyns, *Chinese Art, the Minor Arts*, Pl. 160

PLATE LXXVIII

CONTAINER IN THE SHAPE OF A CLUSTER OF FUNGI, LILY AND PERSIMMONS

White and red (Chalcedony, partly cornelian)
Mid-Late Ch'ing period (18th-19th century A.D.)
L. 10 1/4 in.   B65 J5

Agate and cornelian, which are varieties of chalcedony, were used starting at least from the 18th century to produce color effects that jade could not offer. In this sense, such stones, like lapis lazuli, rock crystal, turquoise, coral and unlike serpentine, chloromelanite, malachite, chrysoprase, soapstone or other varieties of chalcedony do not duplicate jade. They add a brilliant touch to its already prodigious possibilities.

This curious object is a prime example of the quasi-rococo style which flourished during the late 18th and 19th century China. A rocky formation shows the same cubistic tendencies that one sees in the work of a few contemporaneous painters. It is flanked by a small oval box and gives support to several sprawling shoots of *ling-chih* fungus, this omnipresent motif of Ming and post Ming China,[1] and on the far right by a large lily. Higher up a branch of persimmon links two elements of the rocks. The flat lid of the box is topped by a fungiform *ch'ih* which takes us one step further from the fungus bearer of the preceding plate.

All the elements of this sculpture are carved in the round and from the same chunk of stone. It would be difficult to produce a more convincing illustration of the Chinese lapidaries' genius for exploiting the chromatic possibilities of their stones.

The initiated will easily decipher here a symbolic message emanating from a play upon homonyms. In the national language the lily is known as *pai-ho*, the first syllable of which means also "hundred", the persimmon is *shih* which also means "thing" and the fungus is assimilated to the sceptre *ju-i* meaning also "as (you) wish". So that the combination of these three plants means: "(may) the hundred things (i.e. everything) be as you wish"[2]

(1) Cf. Pls. XLIII, LXIII, LXIV, LXVI and LXXIX
(2) See Nozaki N. "*Kisshō Zuan Kaidai, Shina Fūzoku no Ichi Kenkyū*", Tientsin, 1928, pp. 14 and 15. See also Pls. XLII, XLIV, XLVIII, LXI and LXXI.

Plate LXXIX

JU-I SCEPTRE AND BOWL

White, green and mauve
Late Ch'ing period (19th century A.D.*)*
Respectively 14 in. in length and 5 3/4 in. in diameter   *B60 J483 and B60 J188*

Throughout the 19th century and until only a few decades ago some of the best Peking workshops remained faithful to the Ch'ien Lung tradition. Their material of predilection was Burmese jadeite, which can take a highly vitreous polish. This period is less noted for its creativity than for its technical achievements.

The term *ju-i* (literally "as [you] wish") and the sceptre associated with it have a long history in both Taoist and Buddhist symbolisms.[1] According to one theory the object was derived from the fungus of immortality (*ling-chih*).[2] It is obviously this theory which is illustrated here. In keeping with the traditional love of the Chinese for ambiguity and hybridity[3] the head of the sceptre is simultaneously a cluster of fungi and the head of some conventionalized, mouthless, nondescript animal. Simultaneously, the silhouette of *ju-i* sceptres and especially the profile of their handles recall those of Warring States and Han belt-hooks.[4]

The decoration of the bowl stands in low relief and is much less enigmatic. It consists of a pug-faced Buddhist lion playing with a ball. This brocaded ball, with its peony pattern and its "spirit flying" streamers, may have been originally a symbol of the sun and is frequently regarded as a variant of the "flaming pearl" usually associated with dragons.[5] Part of the tail of the lion and part of the ball are "folded" over the mouthrim of the ball as though they were made of cloth. This analogy is not a gratuitous one since this motif was in all likelihood directly borrowed from contemporaneous tapestries and embroideries.

Published: B60 J483: Gump, *Jade, Stone of Heaven*, Pl. 7

(1) See Pls. XLII, XLIII, LIX, LXIII, LXIV and LXXVIII.
(2) Cf. Williams, *Outlines of Chinese Symbolism and Art Motives*, p. 239.
(3) See for instance Pls. VII, XVI, XVIII, XXV, XXVII, etc.
(4) Cf. Pl. XVI.
(5) See Pl. LXXII.

PLATE LXXX

VASE WITH SUSPENSION

White and green jadeite
Late Ch'ing period (18th-19th century A.D.*)*
China B60 J24+

The placing of a vase on the back of animals was originally a Bronze Age concept.[1] Revived during the Sung period the theme reached its apogee during the later part of the Ch'ing dynasty when it is reproduced in an infinity of variations in many different materials including jade.

The bird (a sort of elaborated phoenix), the vase, the chain and the swing handle were all carved from one single piece of jadeite. This astonishing contraption is typical of the tours de force which made the reputation of the best of the Late Ch'ing workshops.[2]

The vase, itself, is derived from an ancient bronze shape.[3] Its shoulder and collar zones are decorated with monsters' masks and *ju-i* like spirals. The latter motif also appears on the lid. The top of the swing handle is carved in the shape of two confronted dragon heads holding a ring in their mouths. This ring serves as a suspension hole and is probably also a variant of the flaming pearl.[4] The lid is attached to the swing handle by means of a chain made of nine double links.

The bird is almost all feathers. It seems to be equipped with four different tails, one of which, a multi-branched one, curves back all the way under the body between the legs and reaches the breast. The wings, the most archaistic detail so far as the bird is concerned, seem to have a life of their own. They suggest one of those arched phoenixes that were typical of the Warring States period.[5] The main bird holds a lotus flower in its beak and an additional ring handle is attached to its neck.

It is this type of translucent emerald green which is referred to as *fei-ts'ui* (literally "kingfisher") by the Chinese and some Western authors since the 18th century.

(1) See for instance Seiichi Mizuno, *Bronzes and Jades of Ancient China*, Tokyo, 1959, Pl. 75
(2) Cf. caption, facing Pl. XLVI
(3) Known as *hu*. See for instance *A.B.C. Bronzes*, Pl. LIV
(4) Cf. Pl. LXII
(5) Cf. Pl. XV

Chronology

THE ANCIENT PERIOD	*ca. 2500 B.C.—2nd century A.D.*
1st stage	
Neolithic	ca. 2500–1500 B.C.
2nd stage	ca. 14th—5th century B.C.
Shang	1523–1028 B.C.
Western Chou	1027–771 B.C.
Ch'un-ch'iu	770–481 B.C.
3rd stage	ca. 5th century—2nd century A.D.
Warring States	480–222 B.C.
Ch'in	221–207 B.C.
Han	206–B.C.—220 A.D.
THE MEDIEVAL PERIOD	*3rd—14th century A.D.*
Early Medieval	3rd—6th century A.D.
The Three Kingdoms	221–265 A.D.
The Six Dynasties	265–589 A.D.
Sui	589–618 A.D.
Mid Medieval	7th—10th century A.D.
T'ang	618–906 A.D.
The Five Dynasties	906–960 A.D.
Late Medieval	11th—14th century A.D.
Sung	960-1279 A.D.
Yüan	1279–1368 A.D.
THE MODERN PERIOD	*15th—20th century A.D.*
1st stage	15th—17th century A.D.
Ming	1368–1644 A.D.
Early Ch'ing	17th century A.D.
2nd stage	
Mid Ch'ing	18th century A.D.
3rd stage	
Late Ch'ing	19th century A.D.
Republic	1912–

Key to Abbreviations

Ball, *Decorative motives of Oriental art.*

Ball, Katherine M.
Decorative motives of Oriental art. London, John Lane; New York, Dodd, Mead [1927]

d'Argencé, *A.B.C. ceramics.*

d'Argencé, René-Yvon Lefebvre.
Chinese ceramics in the Avery Brundage Collection. [San Francisco] Published by The de Young Museum Society, dist. by Diablo Press, Berkeley [1967]

d'Argencé, *A.B.C. Chinese art treasures.*

d'Argencé, René-Yvon Lefebvre.
Chinese treasures from the Avery Brundage Collection [catalogue of an exhibition] New York, The Asia Society, dist. by New York Graphic Society, 1968.

d'Argencé, *A.B.C. Chinese bronzes.*

d'Argencé, René-Yvon Lefebvre.
Ancient Chinese bronzes in the Avery Brundage Collection. Berkeley, Published by Diablo Press for the deYoung Museum Society [1966]

d'Argencé, *Apollo.*

d'Argencé, René-Yvon Lefebvre.
Chinese jades from Shang to Ch'ing [in the Avery Brundage Collection] *Apollo* n.s. 84: 134–9. August 1966.

d'Argencé, *Asia Foundation.*

d'Argencé, René-Yvon Lefebvre.
The Avery Brundage Collection of Asian art. IN *The Asia Foundation. Program Bulletin* no. 40: Aug. 1966, pp. 3–11. (Special issue)

d'Argencé, *Propyläen.*

Fontein, Jan und Rose Hempel.
China, Korea, Japan. Mit Beiträgen von Yvon d'Argencé [and others] Berlin, Propyläen Verlag, 1968. (Propyläen Kunstgeschichte [2nd ed.] Band 17)

Donnelly, *The animal in Chinese art.*

Donnelly, P. J.
Catalogue of an exhibition of the animal in Chinese art. Organized by The Arts Council of Great Britain and the Oriental Ceramic Society, June 19th to July 19th 1968 at the Arts Council Gallery...London. London, The Oriental Ceramic Society, 1968.

Garner, *Oriental blue and white.*

Garner, *Sir* Harry.
Oriental blue and white. London, Faber and Faber [1954]

Gump, *Jade, stone of heaven.*

Gump, Richard.
Jade, stone of heaven. Garden City, N. Y., Doubleday [1962]

Gure, *Selected examples.*

Gure, Desmond.
Selected examples from the jade exhibition at Stockholm, 1963; a comparative study. The Museum of Far Eastern Antiquities, Stockholm. Bulletin No. 36, pp. 117–158.

Hansford, *Chinese carved jade.*

Hansford, S. Howard.
Chinese carved jade. Greenwich, Conn., New York Graphic Society [1968]

Hansford, *Chinese jade carving.*

Hansford, S. Howard.
Chinese jade carving. [London] Lund Humphries, 1950.

Hansford, *Jade, essence of hills and streams.* | *Jade, the essence of hills and streams.* New York, American Elsevier Pub. Co. [1969]

Hartman, *Chinese jade of five centuries.* | Hartman, Joan. *Chinese jade of five centuries.* Rutland, Vt.; Tokyo, Japan, C.E. Tuttle [1969]

Jenyns and Watson, *Chinese art, the minor arts.* | Jenyns, R. Soame and William Watson. *Chinese art, the minor arts...*2 v. New York, Universe Books, 1963 and 1965.

Jenyns, *Later Chinese porcelain.* | Jenyns, R. Soame. *Later Chinese porcelain; the Ch'ing dynasty (1644–1912).* 3rd ed. London, Faber and Faber [1965]

Jenyns, *Ming pottery and porcelain.* | Jenyns, R. Soame. *Ming pottery and porcelain.* London, Faber and Faber [1953]

Loo, *Chinese archaic jades.* | Loo (C.T.) & Co., New York. *An exhibition of Chinese archaic jades, arranged for Norton Gallery of Art*, West Palm Beach, Florida, 1950. New York, C.T. Loo, Inc. [n.d.]

Mayers, *Manual.* | Mayers, William F. *The Chinese reader's manual.* Shanghai, The Presbyterian Mission Press, 1910.

Nozaki, *Kisshō zuan kaidai.* | Nozaki, Nobuchika.

吉 祥 圖 案 解 題 （支 那 風 俗 の 一 研 究） 野 崎 誠 近 著， 再 版， 東 京， 平 凡 社， 昭 和 15 年 (1940). 2 v.

Osaka, *San Francisco exchange exhibition.* | San Francisco.   Center of Asian Art and Culture. *Osaka exchange exhibition; paintings from the Abe Collection and other masterpieces of Chinese art.* [San Francisco] Osaka Municipal Museum of Fine Arts and San Francisco Center of Asian Art and Culture [1970]

Rawson and Ayers, *Chinese Jade* | Jessica Rawson and John Ayers. *Chinese jade throughout the ages*, Catalogue of an exhibition organized by The Arts Council of Great Britain and the Oriental Ceramic Society, London 1975.

Salmony, *Carved Jade* | Salmony, Alfred. *Carved jade of ancient China.* Berkeley, Gillick Press, 1938.

Salmony, *Chinese jade.* | Salmony, Alfred. *Chinese jade through the Wei dynasty.*   New York, The Ronald Press [1963]

T.O.C.S. | *Transactions of the Oriental Ceramic Society*, London.

Williams, *Outlines.* | Williams, C.A.S. *Outlines of Chinese symbolism and art motives.* Shanghai, Kelly and Walsh, 1932.

Selected Bibliography

Anhwei, China (Province). Wen Wu Kuan Li Yüan Hui.

壽縣蔡侯墓出土遺物. 安徽省文物管理委員會. 安徽省博物館編著. 中國科學院考古研究所編輯. 北京, 科學出版社, 1956. (考古學專刊乙種第 5 號)

Archaic jades in the Pillsbury collection.
Minneapolis Institute of Arts. Bulletin 19: 68–70. April 5, 1930.

Ardenne de Tizac, Henri Jean d'.
"Les jades classique" *Revue des Arts Asiatiques* 1: 10–20. May, 1924.

Ball, Katherine M.
Decorative motives of Oriental art. London, John Lane; New York, Dodd, Mead [1927]

Barlow, *Sir* James Alan.
Chinese ceramics, bronzes and jades in the collection of Sir Alan and Lady Barlow, by Michael Sullivan. London, Faber and Faber, 1963.

Beurdeley, Michel.
The Chinese collector through the centuries; from the Han to the 20th century. [Translated from the French: *"L'Amateur chinois des Han au XXe siècle"* by Diana Imber] Rutland, Vt.; Tokyo, Japan, C. E. Tuttle [1966]

Bishop, Heber Reginald.
The Heber R. Bishop collection of jade and other hard stones. [New York] The Metropolitan Museum of Art [1906]

Bishop, Heber Reginald.
Investigations and studies in jade. The Bishop Collection. New York, Privately printed, 1906. 2v. (weight: 111.5 lbs.)

British Museum. Dept. of Oriental Antiquities and of Ethnography.
Chinese archaic jades in the British Museum, by Soame Jenyns. [London] The Trustees of the British Museum, 1951.

Buhot, Jean.
L'exposition de jades au Musée Cernuschi [a report of an exhibition] *Revue des Arts Asiatiques* 4: 110–11. June 1927.

Bushell, Stephen W.
Carving in jade and other hard stones. IN HIS Chinese art. 2nd ed. London, HMSO, 1921. vol. 1, pp. 120+.

Chang, Hung Chao. 章 鴻 釗
Lapidarium sinicum, a study of the rocks, fossils and metals as known in Chinese literature. 2nd ed., rev. Peking [The Geological Survey of China] 1927. (The Geological Survey of China. Memoirs, ser. B, no. 2) Text in Chinese. Chinese title: 石雅.

Ch'en, Chiu Ts'ao.

上海玉雕. 陳秋草編. 上海, 上海人民美術出版社, 1957.

Cheng, Te K'un.
Jade carving. IN HIS *Archaeology in China.* vol. III, *Chou China.* Cambridge, England, W. Heffer & Sons, 1963. pp. 183–199.

Cheng, Te K'un.
Jade carving. IN HIS *Archaeology in China.* vol. II, *Shang China.* Cambridge, England, W. Heffer & Sons, 1960. pp. 109–125.

Cheng, Te K'un.
"T'ang and Ming jades." *Oriental Ceramic Society. Transactions* 28: 23–35. 1953–54.

Chicago. Art Institute.
Archaic Chinese jades from the Edward and Louise B. Sonnenschein collection. [Catalogue] by Alfred Salmony. [Chicago] 1952.

Chu, Te Jun, 1294–1365, comp.

古玉圖. 朱德潤［字］澤民 1294-1365 撰. 清乾隆壬申 (1752). 天都黃氏亦政堂刊本
一冊一函.

Damour, M. A.
Nouvelles analyses sur la jadéite et sur quelques roches sodifères. *Annales de Chimie et de Physique*
5 série, 24. 1881.

d'Argencé, René-Yvon Lefebvre.
Ancient Chinese bronzes in the Avery Brundage Collection. Berkeley, Published by Diablo
Press for the de Young Museum Society [1966]

d'Argencé, René-Yvon Lefebvre.
"The Avery Brundage Collection of Asian art." IN *The Asia Foundation.* *Program Bulletin*
40: 3–11. August 1966. (Special issue)

d'Argencé, René-Yvon Lefebvre.
Chinese ceramics in the Avery Brundage Collection. [San Francisco] Published by The
de Young Museum Society, distributed by Diablo Press, Berkeley [1967]

d'Argencé, René-Yvon Lefebvre.
"Chinese jades from Shang to Ch'ing in the Avery Brundage Collection." *Apollo* n.s.
84: 134–9. August 1966.

d'Argencé, René-Yvon Lefebvre.
Chinese treasures from the Avery Brundage Collection [catalogue of an exhibition] New York,
The Asia Society, distributed by New York Graphic Society, 1968.

David, Madeleine.
Sculptures et jades à l'exposition des arts de la Chine. *Cahiers d'Art* 12: 211–15. 1937.

Dohrenwend, Doris
Chinese jades in the Royal Ontario Museum, Toronto 1971.

Donnelly, P. J.
Catalogue of an exhibition of the animal in Chinese art. Organized by The Arts Council of
Great Britain and The Oriental Ceramic Society, June 19th to July 19th 1968 at The
Arts Council Gallery . . . London. London, The Oriental Ceramic Society, 1968.

Ecke, Gustav.
Early Chinese jades selected from Alfred Salmony's posthumous works. *Connoisseur* (American
ed.) 147: 61–7. March 1961.

Eumorfopoulos, George.
*The George Eumorfopoulos collection: catalogue of the Chinese and Corean bronzes, sculpture,
jades, jewellery, and miscellaneous objects,* by W. Percival Yetts . . . 3v. London, E. Benn,
1929–32.

Exhibition of Islamic jades at the Victoria and Albert Museum.
Oriental Art n.s. 12(3): 202–3. Autumn 1966.

Fontein, Jan.
China, Korea, Japan, von Jan Fontein und Rose Hempel. Mit Beiträgen von Yvon d'Ar-
gencé [and others] Berlin, Propyläen Verlag, 1968. (*Propyläen Kunstgeschichte* [*2nd ed.*]
Band 17)

Gieseler, G.
Le jade dans le culte et les rites funéraires en Chine sous les dynasties Tcheou et Han. *Revue
Archéologique* 4: 118. July 1916.

Gieseler, G.
Les symboles de jade dans le Taoisme. *Revue de l'Histoire des Religions.* 1932.

Gorer, Edgar and J.F. Blacker.
Chinese porcelain and hard stones. 2v. London, B. Quaritch, 1911.

Gump, Richard.
Jade, stone of heaven. Garden City, N. Y., Doubleday, 1962.

Gure, Desmond.
"An early [Chinese] jade animal vessel and some parallels." *Oriental Ceramic Society. Transactions* 31: 75–82. 1957–59.

Gure, Desmond.
"Jades of the Sung group." *Oriental Ceramic Society. Transactions* 32: 39–50. 1959–60.

Gure, Desmond.
"Notes on the identification of jade." *Oriental Art* 3(3): 115–120. 1951.

Gure, Desmond.
"Selected examples from the jade exhibition at Stockholm, 1963; a comparative study." *The Museum of Far Eastern Antiquities. Bulletin* 36: 117–158. 1964.

Gure, Desmond.
"Some unusual early jades and their dating." *Oriental Ceramic Society. Transactions* 33: 41–59. 1960–62.

Gustaf Adolf, *Crown Prince of Sweden*, 1882–
Selected Chinese antiquities from the collection of Gustaf Adolf, Crown Prince of Sweden. Edited by Nils Palmgren. Stockholm, Generalstabens Litografiska Anstalts Förlag, 1948.

Hansford, S. Howard.
Chinese carved jade. Greenwich, Conn., New York Graphic Society [1968]

Hansford, S. Howard.
Chinese jade carving. London, Lund Humphries, 1950.

Hansford, S. Howard.
"The disposition of ritual jades in royal burials of the Chou dynasty." *Royal Asiatic Society. Journal* pts. 3–4: 138–42. 1949.

Hansford, S. Howard.
"Jade and jade carving in the Ch'ing dynasty." *Oriental Ceramic Society. Transactions* 35: 29–40. 1963–64.

Hansford, S. Howard.
"Jade and the kingfisher." *Oriental Art* 1(1): 12–17. 1948.

Hansford, S. Howard.
Jade, the essence of hills and streams; the von Oertzen collection of Chinese and Indian jades. New York, American Elsevier Pub. Co. [1969]

Hardinge, *Sir* Charles.
Jade, fact and fable. London, Published for the Gulbenkian Museum, School of Oriental Studies, University of Durham by Luzac & Co., 1961.

Hartman, Joan M.
Chinese jade of five centuries. Rutland, Vt.; Tokyo, Japan, C. E. Tuttle [1969]

Hartman, Joan M.
Ancient Chinese jades from the Buffalo Museum of Science, New York, Published by China House Gallery, China Institute in America, 1975.

Huang, Chün.
衡齋藏見古玉圖. 黃濬, 撰集者. 北平, 各省大書局 [1935]

Huang, Chün.
古玉圖錄初集. 黃濬, 撰集者. 北平, 各省大書局 [1939]

Huang, Chün.
鄴中片羽. 黃濬 [著] [antiquities from An-Yang] 北平 [1935]

Jenyns, R. Soame and William Watson.
Chinese art, the minor arts . . . 2v. New York, Universe Books, 1963 and 1965.

K'ao Ku Hsüeh Pao. [periodical]
(*Kaogu Xuebao*)
考古學報. 北京, 中國科學院考古研究所, 1936–
Title changed to *K'ao Ku* with the January, 1959 issue.

K'ao Ku T'ung Hsün. [periodical]
(Kaogu Tongxun)

考古通訊. 北京, 科學出版社, 1957–

Kelley, Charles F.
"Loan exhibition of Jade." *Chicago Art Institute. Bulletin* 31: 82–86. November 1937.

Kelley, Charles F.
"Sonnenschein jade collection at Chicago Art Institute." *Chicago Art Institute. Quarterly* 46: 49–54. September 1952.

Kuwayama, George
Chinese jade from southern California collections, Los Angeles, Los Angeles County Museum of Art, 1976.

Laufer, Berthold.
Archaic Chinese jades collected in China by A. W. Bahr. New York, Privately printed for A. W. Bahr, 1927.

Laufer, Berthold.
Jade, a study in Chinese archaeology and religion. South Pasadena, P. D. and Ione Perkins in cooperation with The Westwood Press and W. M. Hawley, 1946. (Originally published as Field Museum of Natural History, Chicago. Publication no. 154. Anthro. series vol. 10. Chicago, 1910)

Laufer, Berthold.
Le jade dans le culte et les rites funéraires en Chine sous les dynasties Tcheou et Han (G. Gieseler). *Revue Archéologique* 5x., IV, p. 61. 1916.

Laufer, Berthold.
"Jade fish symbols in China." *Open Court* 24: 673–80. November 1912.

Laufer, Berthold.
"Two Chinese Imperial jades." *Fine Arts Journal* p. 236–41. June 1915.

Lee, Sherman E. and Wai-kam Ho.
Chinese art under the Mongols: the Yüan dynasty (1279–1368) [catalogue of an exhibition. Cleveland] The Cleveland Museum of Art [1968]

Lion-Goldschmidt, Daisy.
Jade. IN *Chinese art,* by Daisy Lion-Goldschmidt and Jean-Claude Moreau-Gobard. New York, Universe Books, 1960. pp. 133–195.

Loehr, Max.
Ancient Chinese jades from the Grenville L. Winthrop collection, Cambridge, 1975.

London. International Exhibition of Chinese Art, 1935–6.
Catalogue . . . London, Royal Academy of Arts [1935?]

London. International Exhibition of Chinese Art, 1935–6.
Jade. IN *Illustrated catalogue of Chinese government exhibits for the International Exhibition of Chinese Art in London. Vol. IV, Miscellaneous.* Shanghai, 1937. pp. 33–68.

Loo (C.T.), et cie.
Jades archaïques de Chine appartenant à M. C.T. Loo, publiés par M. Paul Pelliot. Paris et Bruxelles, G. van Oest, 1925.

Loo (C.T.) & Co., New York.
An exhibition of Chinese jades . . . arranged for Norton Gallery of Art, West Palm Beach, Florida, January 20 to March 1, 1950. New York, C. T. Loo, Inc., [n.d.]

Los Angeles (County). Museum.
The arts of the T'ang dynasty; a loan exhibition organized by the Los Angeles County Museum from collections in America, the Orient and Europe, January 8-February 17, 1957. Introduction by Henry Trubner. Los Angeles, 1957.

Lung, Ta Yüan.
古玉圖譜. 龍大淵. First issued in 1175 under instruction of Ch'un Hsi, an Emperor of Sung. Published again in 1779 by Chiang Ch'un.

Michel, Henri.
"Les jades astronomiques chinois." *Bulletin des Musées Royaux d'Art et d'Histoire* (Brussels) S. 4 v. 19: 31–8. January 1947.

Mizuno, Seiichi.
　"A Han jade found in a stone-cist tomb at Liao-yang, South Manchuria." *Toho Gakuho*
　no. 4, 1933.

Mizuno, Seiichi.
　殷周青銅器と玉. 水野清一著. 東京, 日本経済新聞社, 昭和34年 (1959).

Needham, Joseph.
　"Jade and abrasives." IN HIS *Science and civilization in China.* vol. 3. Cambridge,
　Cambridge University Press, 1959. pp. 663–669.

New York. Arden Gallery.
　3000 years of Chinese jade . . . January 19th through February 11, 1939. New York [The
　Arden Gallery, 1939]

Nott, Stanley Charles.
　Chinese jades in the Stanley Charles Nott collection. West Palm Beach, Fla., The author,
　1942.

Oriental Ceramic Society, London.
　Catalogue of the exhibition of Chinese jades from April 14th to June 9th, 1948. Introduction by
　S. Howard Hansford. IN *Oriental Ceramic Society. Transactions* 23: 46–61. 1947–48.
　(Also published as a seperatum.)

Osgood, Cornelius.
　Blue-and-white Chinese porcelain; a study of form. New York, Ronald Press Co. [1956]

Palmer, J. P.
　Jade. London, Spring Books, 1967.

Pelliot, Paul.
　"Note on the Ku Yü T'u P'u, 'recueil de faux.' " *T'oung Pao* 29: 199. 1932.

Pennsylvania. University. Museum.
　Archaic Chinese jades, special exhibition, February 1940. Philadelphia, [n.d.]

Pope-Hennessy, Una.
　Early Chinese jades. New York, Stokes; London, E. Benn, 1923.

R.M.H.
　"Jades from the collection of Wu Ta Ch'eng." *Toronto. University. Royal Ontario
　Museum. Bulletin* 9: 9–11. January 1930.

Salmony, Alfred.
　"A Chinese jade bear of the early Han period." *Artibus Asiae* 10(4): 257–65. 1947.

Salmony, Alfred.
　"The identification of an ancient Chinese jade." *Journal of the Indian Society of Oriental Art*
　15:(1): 77–83. 1947.

Salmony, Alfred.
　"Jades archaïques chinois." *Cahiers d'Art* year 6, no. 7–8: 341–7. 1931.

Salmony, Alfred.
　"Ein Jadeschmuck der chinesischen Frühzeit"; with English translation. *Pantheon* 10:
　292–4. sup. 70. Sept. 1932.

Salmony, Alfred.
　"Die Stellung des Jades in der chinesischen Kunst." *Chinesisch-Deutscher Almanach.* 1931.

Savage, George.
　Chinese jade, a concise introduction. New York, October House [1965]

Schneeberger, Pierre, F.
　The Baur collection, Geneva, Chinèse jades and other hard stones, Geneva, Collections Baur,
　1976.

Seligman, Charles G.
　The Seligman collection of Oriental art. London, Published for the Arts Council of Great
　Britain by L. Humphries, 1957– v. 1. *Chinese, Central Asian and Luristan bronzes and
　Chinese jades and sculptures,* by S. H. Hansford.

Sickman, L. and A. Soper.
  The art and architecture of China. 3rd ed. [Baltimore] Penguin Books [1968]

Smith College. Museum of Art.
  Archaic Chinese jades. Mr. and Mrs. Ivan B. Hart collection. Catalogue by Elizabeth Lyons. Northampton, Mass., 1963.

Sugimura, Yuzo.
  Chinese sculpture, bronzes and jades in Japanese collections. Honolulu, East-West Center Press [1966]

Trousdale, W. B.
  "Chinese jade at Philadelphia." *Oriental Art* n.s. 10(2): 107–14. Summer 1964.

Ueno, Seiichi.
  有竹齋藏古玉譜. 上野精一. (the early Chinese jades in the collection of the late Riichi Uyeno) [n.p.] 大正十四年 (1925).

Umehara, Sueji.
  洛陽金村古墓聚英. 梅原末治 [著] 京都, 小林寫眞製版所出版部 [1936]

Umehara, Sueji.
  河南安陽遺物の研究. 梅原末治 [編] 京都, 桑名文星堂, 昭和十六年 (1941).

Umehara, Sueji.
  洛陽金村古墓聚英 (增訂). 京都, 小林出版部, 昭和十八年 (1943).

Umehara, Sueji.
  支那古玉圖錄. 梅原末治 [編] 京都, 桑名文星堂, [1955]

Venice. Palazzo Ducale.
  Mostra d'arte cinese; catalogo. Settimo centenario di Marco Polo, 1954. [Venice] Alfieri Editore [1954]

Wang, Ta Lung.
  陶齋古玉圖. 王大隆, 欣夫編纂. 民國二十五年 (1936). 上海來青閣影印.

Watson, William.
  "Archaic Chinese jades." *Apollo* 52: 80–3+. Sept. 1950.

Watson, William.
  "Chinese jade after the Han dyansty." *Apollo* 53: 99–104. April 1951.

Welch, Stuart C.
  The art of Mughal India; painting and precious objects [catalogue of an exhibition] New York, The Asia Society, distributed by H. N. Abrams [1963]

Wen Wu. [periodical]
  文物. 北京, 一. No. 1, 1950–

White, William C.
  Tombs of old Lo-Yang. Shanghai, Kelly and Walsh, 1934.

Wills, Geoffrey.
  Jade of the East, New York, Tokyo, Hong Kong, Weatherhill/Orientations, 1972.

Wu, Ta Ch'eng.
  古玉圖考. 吳大澂 [著] 上海, 同文書局石印本, 清光緒十五年 (1889).

Yamanaka and Company.
  Various illustrated catalogues describing jades. See especially 1927, 1930, 1933, 1935.

Yetts, W. Percival.
  "Some Chinese jades and a bronze". *Burlington Magazine* 49: 94–97. 1926.

Yetts, W. Percival.
  Symbolism in Chinese art. [Leyden, Holland, Printed by E. J. Brill, 1912]